BEFORE YOU START making decisions about decorating your home or buying furniture and equipment, take a good, long look at your lifestyle. For example, are you living solo or with a partner? Do you have young family or teenage children, or an elderly relation living with you? Are you a student sharing with four others, trying to squeeze into a two-bedroom flat? When sharing you will almost certainly have to sacrifice some personal wishes in order to come up with the best solution for everybody in the group. However, this is the time to imagine perfect solutions and ideal environments. At this stage you can be as aspiring as you like.

Consider your personality—are you outgoing and gregarious or studious and solitary? Will you be doing your own cooking or mostly eating out? Are you a fitness fanatic with exercise equipment and special clothes to find room for? Are you a romantic who loves scented baths and satin bed linen? Do you want to luxuriate in a king-size bed? All these things will affect how you arrange and furnish your home. This is the moment to think about who you are and how you'd like to live.

Assessing your needs

Lifestyle: the way you'd like to live

Throughout the centuries many different design styles have evolved, most of which have survived in some form as models for today's interiors. Some people living in traditional homes take pleasure in decorating and furnishing them exactly as they would have been in the past. Others are happy to reproduce the "look" of a past style, and many modern paints, wallpapers, and fabrics are based on designs taken from the past using slightly different pattern sizes or colorways to fit in with today's tastes. Some people prefer a more eclectic approach, putting together elements from various styles or countries to make a highly personal and unique style of their own. It's worth spending some time pinpointing your preferred style so that your home will have a coordinated look, as this will always help to make the spaces seem larger than they really are. Don't think about each room in isolation from the rest of the house. Open doors give a vista to other rooms, halls, or passages, and these should all harmonize. The styles suggested below are very generalized. If you want a more precise style, such as Biedermeier (a sturdy yet elegant style from the Napoleonic wars) or Gustavian (an 18th-century Swedish equivalent to the English Georgian style), then researching it can be fascinating and rewarding.

Right A glamorous living room that manages to introduce an element of modern simplicity. This is achieved by combining a luxurious throw on the sofa and a soft, fluffy rug on the floor with an elegant square fireplace, simple picture frames, and understated white walls.

Historic

THE LOOK There's a large choice here, from the timeless English Country look, built up over centuries, to Tudor and Gothic, Georgian, American Country and Colonial, French Provincial, Victorian, Arts and Crafts, or 20th Century. You could be specific and go for a retro 1930s style such as Bauhaus or Art Deco, or embrace the general timeless country look of floral chintzes, cabinet-maker upholstery, and overall comfort.

THE FURNITURE The furniture in all these styles is usually simple, beautifully made, and of wood, the chairs and settees plumply upholstered. They may have loose covers, or have "throws" draped over them.

THE SPACES Use of space relies on a careful but informal arrangement of good quality furniture and fabrics, seemingly casual but carefully thought out. The kitchen should have plenty of wooden surfaces, plus a kitchen table with drawers.

Modernist

THE LOOK Modernist is an uncompromising style that won't mix or match easily with traditional styles. It was started in the 1920s and continues to be popular, its simplicity and restrained look fitting in well with today's rather fast pace of life and smaller interiors. It is summed up well by the phrase "less is more."

THE FURNITURE Furniture shapes are strikingly simple, often surprisingly comfortable, but not usually upholstered. Leather-covered sofas in boxy shapes, and stark industrial materials such as tubular steel furniture and glass tables are all appropriate for this book.

THE SPACES Objects such as television sets, music systems, records, and books are all hidden away. Pictures and other decorative objects are displayed one at a time, if at all. In fact there are no unnecessary bits of furniture, curtains, or objects on show.

Regional

THE LOOK Regional styles are based on timeless peasant or country styles that have evolved from local vernacular architecture, materials, and craft skills. They include: Mediterranean (particularly from Greece and the South of France); Nomadic (particularly Middle Eastern tribal peoples); Japanese (although this could equally well fit in with the Modernist look); Indian; and Latin American and Caribbean, with their uninhibited colors.

THE FURNITURE Simple furnishings rely on color and hand-craftsmanship using local materials such as wood or rattan and cane, or woven rugs such as kilims or dhurries laid on the floor or used as cushion covers for seating.

THE SPACES Nothing is fitted. In many of these regional areas much of life is spent outside, so furniture is sparse. There are open shelves in the kitchen and rooms are usually small, so the less furniture the better.

Glamorous

THE LOOK This is often based on the fairy-tale interiors produced in the Hollywood films of the twentieth century. Materials are plush, shiny, slinky, and expensive. Curtains are lined, ruched, swagged, and heavy. Beds are king- or emperor-sized and carpets inches deep. Ornate mirrors reflect and enhance the overall effect of sumptuous unreality.

THE FURNITURE There is no particular style for the furniture as long as it is large, imposing, and probably leather-covered. The bed should be not only big enough for a giant but also covered in silk or satin.

THE SPACES Since the whole look is designed to present the unattainable, the sizes of the rooms are usually enormous. Luckily, mirrors are a great part of this look and they can be used to enhance the size of even a small room, particularly when carefully placed to produce never-ending reflections.

Mirrors reflect and enhance the overall effect of sumptuous unreality. They can be used to enhance the size of even a small room, particularly when carefully placed to produce never-ending reflections.

Lifestyle: the way you live

Assessing your lifestyle can be revealing and often surprising. You may not realize how much time you actually spend in your home. If you have small children it's more important to have a generous play space where they can enjoy themselves and learn through play, than to live in an ultra-organized and tidy environment. If you are out for much of the day you will be less likely to accumulate clutter, so you will need less storage space and have more opportunity for the stylish display of artworks or collections of various kinds. If you work from home you will want to incorporate your working or office space into the general style of your home, unless you have the luxury of dedicating a room solely to your work. The gregarious and party-minded will require spacious clothes storage, while the hospitable will want a home that is welcoming, with a carefully organized layout that creates a feeling of spaciousness, no matter how small. Use the checklist opposite to pinpoint your own needs.

"

You may not realize how much time you spend in your home. The hospitable will want a home that is welcoming, with a carefully organized layout that creates a feeling of spaciousness, no matter how small.

"

Below If you are in all day you need to use every inch, including space under the stairs for compact storage. Here a useful blanket chest also doubles up as seating.

Below right Even with two clothes fans, you can still organize a small space with wit and style by using rails at different heights and being disciplined about putting clothes away.

CHECKLIST

WHAT YOU NEED

- A ship's galley-style kitchen ☐
- Informal comfortable kitchen ☐
- Kitchen "niche" in living room ☐
- Unfitted style ☐
- Breakfast bar ☐
- Sleek fitted units ☐
- Latest gadgets ☐
- Catering-style equipment ☐
- Kitchen/dining room ☐
- Separate dining area ☐
- Formal dining room ☐
- Generous food storage ☐
- Child-friendly kitchen ☐
- Large fridge/freezer ☐
- Kitchen/dining table ☐
- Enclosed storage ☐
- Open or dresser-style storage ☐

CROSS REFER TO

- All day at home pp.14–16
- Out all day pp.16–17
- Dual-purpose rooms (kitchen/dining) p.39 ● Living and entertaining p.64–7
- Eating pp.72–5 ● How to create the illusion pp.118–19

Bathing

Your idea of the perfect bathroom may include an enormous circular bath, sumptuous ceramic tiles, and mirroring everywhere. In the modern small home you are unlikely to achieve this, but you can still get that feeling of pampered luxury provided there is enough room to use the facilities comfortably and the room is warm and well ventilated.

Small bathrooms do present a design challenge. They must be functional while managing to combine a constricted space with that all-important sense of luxury. For many people the bathtub itself is unnecessary, taking up valuable space when a shower will do just as well. However, others enjoy a good soak in the bath and if you are determined to include one there are numerous designs on the market, many specifically for small bathrooms. Bath-and-shower combinations can save space, and shower cubicles come in many sizes, shapes, and materials. It is important to go for good quality; water is a great destroyer and cheap materials will rust or crack and get dirty.

> Small bathrooms do present a design challenge. They must be functional while managing to combine a constricted space with that all-important sense of luxury.

Solo Living

ESSENTIAL Style and comfort are the two basic necessities and, no matter how small your bathroom, there are stylish bathroom fittings that will help you create these. You may have to choose between a bath and a walk-in shower, but a shower head can be fitted over a small bath and screened by a panel.

DESIRABLE A dual-purpose radiator/heated towel rail is a very desirable item. There are some highly sculptural designs on the market, in a choice of chrome or bright and cheerful colors, that can enhance the look and comfort of a bathroom considerably.

STORAGE One person may not need very much storage space for toiletries but the bathroom can become a good display/storage space for items from other parts of your life. For example, pretty china plates can be hung on the wall, or a high narrow shelf run around the room to hold plates or other items difficult to house elsewhere.

Couples

ESSENTIAL No matter how small the bathroom, you may find you save much nudging and early morning animosity if you have two small washbasins rather than one large one. Very attractive small circular or square basins are available in ceramic or glass, which can sit in a fitted countertop.

DESIRABLE Bidets, like lavatories, take up more space than you might imagine. If a bidet is on your wish list you may find it worth sacrificing a bathtub and installing instead a top-of-the-range shower cubicle.

STORAGE Each person should have a separate shelf for toilet articles. Shelves under the basin can be concealed with fitted cupboard doors in a style of your choice, or with pretty gingham curtains to enhance a cottage look.

Family

ESSENTIAL The bathroom should be large enough to hold at least two people at a time so a parent can supervise bath times. A heated towel rail, or preferably two, will ensure towels don't become mildewy.

DESIRABLE For the tiniest children a baby-changing area is ideal. For toddlers a comparatively low lavatory would be an obvious advantage. Do opt for a simple but cheerful décor and easily cleaned surfaces. Non-slip surfaces are also important.

STORAGE In a largish bathroom you may be able to fit a laundry basket or, better still, a dirty clothes bin as part of a fitted storage system under the sink. It is absolutely essential to have a lockable medicine cabinet out of reach of young children old enough to climb.

Sharing

ESSENTIAL Sharers often have difficulty in deciding who does the cleaning, so a bathroom with built-in fittings, fitted storage, and easily cleaned surfaces is essential. It's also important to have a separate towel rail for each person—if heated, so much the better.

DESIRABLE A shelf for each person for individual teeth-cleaning apparatus and toiletries is ideal. If you have to choose between bath and shower, a shower will usually use less hot water, take up less space, and, importantly, take less time so other sharers don't have to queue up outside the bathroom.

STORAGE Too much storage can be a disadvantage when sharing. A small unit of fitted storage under the basin is a good idea, with a shelf for household cleaning equipment. Storing things other than shaving or teeth-cleaning equipment and soaps is usually not a good idea in a shared house.

CHECKLIST

WHAT YOU NEED

- A bathtub for a really long soak ☐
- A whirlpool or steam bath ☐
- A two-person bath ☐
- A sunken bath ☐
- A combined bath and shower ☐
- A separate bath and shower ☐
- A shower instead of a bath ☐
- Bidet ☐
- Separate WC ☐
- Large medicine cabinet ☐
- Storage for toiletries ☐
- Storage for household cleaning products ☐
- Floor-to-ceiling ceramic tiles ☐
- Heated towel rail(s) ☐
- Glass or stainless steel basin(s) ☐
- Circular or square basin(s) ☐

CROSS REFER TO

- Dual-purpose rooms p.41 ● Tiny spaces pp.46–7 ● Bathroom pp.80–83 ● Linen storage pp.114–15 ● Use of mirrors pp.126–7

Right Creating an alcove can make a snug and comfortable place for one person to sleep, while providing plenty of storage underneath. This is a particularly useful solution for a child's room or a guest bedroom.

Sleeping

The first thing you want in your bedroom is a comfortable bed. Visions of shiny pink satin bedcovers reflected in dozens of mirrors, à la Hollywood, or a medieval oak four poster may be your chosen style, but do make sure you have a good mattress first. Most styles can be adapted to smaller areas; even single beds can be given the open poster or half-tester treatment. A simple Colonial or Shaker style would fit well in a dual-purpose bedroom/ workroom, married with office furniture in varnished wood. Minimalist styles can also easily be adapted to dual-purpose rooms.

If you want a boudoir, where you can get away for a quiet period to write or read or simply relax to music, choose a friendly, intimate style, perhaps with a floral pattern or with country-style checks, with a small armchair, a small computer or writing table, and a low bed (more informal than a high one). If you want the room just for sleeping and dressing, don't pick the best room in the house—any carefully arranged small room will do.

> " The first thing you want in your bedroom is a comfortable bed. Don't necessarily pick the best room in the house— any carefully arranged small room will do. "

Solo Living

STYLE If you live on your own the world is your oyster as far as style goes. But remember that some styles are easier to achieve in a small home than others. Modern minimalist or traditional colonial styles are certainly possible, but the grand romantic styles will be more difficult to make convincing in a tiny room, even with the help of mirrors.

THE BED A tall bed will tend to dominate a small room. It may be better to choose a low divan-type bed that can be used as seating as well. You can always arrange a canopy of muslin or cotton fabric at the back if you want to dress it up.

USES Unless you want the bedroom as a dual-purpose room, why not choose the smallest room in your home and turn it into a really cosy nest. This is much less wasteful of space than choosing a larger room that remains unused during the day.

Couples

STYLE It's not always easy to choose a style that will please both partners. If one of you hankers after frills and florals and the other prefers dark colors and checks what should you do? It shouldn't be beyond the wit of two people to combine both looks into one that will suit both.

THE BED As with style, your requirements for a soft or a firm mattress won't necessarily coincide. Double mattresses are available sprung differently on each side so that each partner can lie comfortably at night.

USES A dual-purpose bedroom/workroom is not easy to arrange with a double bed and storage for two people's clothes and accessories. However, if you have a large enough room, it is best to divide the space with a solid partition such as a bookcase, which will not only seem more deliberate but will also serve as much-needed storage.

Family

STYLE Children will almost certainly want to create their own style, which may not be at all to the liking of their parents. However, it's a good opportunity for children to experiment and learn, and the room can always be altered later. Certainly what they will need is plenty of storage and some desk space.

THE BED It's tempting to buy cheap beds for children but do make sure the mattress is not just cheap foam and that it gives good support. The choice of beds is large, from those with storage or an extra pull-out bed underneath to double bunks for two or single bunks with play space underneath.

USES Young children will usually want to play in the living room near the grown ups. But older children will usually want to escape to a room of their own, which will have to act as bedroom, workroom, and sitting room. Careful planning to allow for the child's particular needs can make this possible.

Sharing

STYLE A shared bedroom will almost certainly be cramped, and the simpler and more compact the furniture and decoration the better. Shaker style is easy to live with and usually practical. The Shaker idea of a rail with pegs all round a room can be used for any item that will hang (including furniture), and can help keep order in the room.

THE BED You might consider installing bunks, of which there are many different styles. This would leave some wall space for perhaps a small desk that could be shared, as well as storage for clothes.

USES In a shared apartment you may need to create a kind of bedsit, where you can work comfortably. The bed doubles up as seating and a unified scheme will give the illusion of space.

CROSS REFER TO

● Anti-hoarding and de-cluttering pp.32–3 ● Studio apartments pp.36–7 ● Attics and basements pp.58–9 ● Bedroom pp.84–7 ● Linen storage pp.114–15 ● Use of mirrors p.126–7

CHECKLIST

WHAT YOU NEED

- Dedicated bedroom
- Dual purpose bed/work room ☐
- Dual purpose bed/play room ☐
- Romantic style ☐
- Minimalist style ☐
- Colonial style ☐
- Hollywood glamour ☐
- Freestanding furniture ☐
- Antique furniture ☐
- Fitted look ☐
- Quiet retreat ☐
- Dual purpose bed/seating ☐
- Mirrored surfaces ☐
- Include washbasin and shower ☐
- Include en suite bathroom ☐
- Bunk bed ☐
- Bed with built-in storage ☐

Clothes enthusiast

Imagine opening a pair of doors and finding a well-lit walk-in closet, in which all your clothes are arranged by color or type, beautifully laundered, and ready to wear. This is, indeed, many women's dream. However, like most people you probably have far too many clothes, some of which you never wear, so your choice of wardrobe and other clothes storage should be carefully selected and planned. This will depend partly on the style of the bedroom, but the things you wear are so diverse in shape and size, and so individual to you, that detailed planning of the storage spaces is important. The particular clothes you wear will dictate the sort of storage they need: long winter coats and business suits with crisply ironed shirts need adequate hanging space if they are to be wearable the next working day; informal clothes can be bundled up for storage but still need drawer or shelf space.

Storage furniture for bedrooms is very versatile. Whether your choice is wall-to-wall, floor-to-ceiling fitted cupboards or a combination of individual small wardrobes and chests of drawers, you should be able to find practical furniture that fits your style and will satisfactorily encompass your range of clothes. Even the most basic cupboard can have a customized fitted interior.

> Your choice of wardrobe and other clothes storage should be carefully selected and planned. The particular clothes you wear will dictate the sort of storage they need.

Solo Living

WORK CLOTHES Your working clothes may be fashionable and tailored. Hanging storage is essential and it's a compact way to hold clothes so you shouldn't need an enormous cupboard. If you have many accessories they can be kept separately in drawers or on shelves.

LEISURE CLOTHES The great thing about informal clothes is that they are usually uncrushable. A couple of shelves in a wardrobe or a low or tall chest of drawers should deal adequately with track suits, T-shirts, jeans, jumpers, and underwear.

SPECIAL CONSIDERATIONS If you collect evening shoes or hats, for example, you will need to consider storage carefully. Hat boxes can be stacked on top of a wardrobe or on a top shelf. Make sure the box is sealed unless you open it frequently, to prevent damage by moths.

Couples

WORK CLOTHES The problem most couples have is dovetailing the requirements of two different people. If you both work in offices, one hanging section of a wardrobe can take both lots of work clothes. However, if one person does manual work and the other works in an office, two separate cupboards should be arranged where outdoor clothes won't spoil tailored, pristine ones.

LEISURE CLOTHES Leisure clothes can be stored together but it will probably be more convenient to have separate chests of drawers so they don't get inextricably mixed up.

SPECIAL CONSIDERATIONS It is a good idea to have a generous laundry box or basket so dirty clothes have a place to go and one person isn't always clearing up after the other.

Family

SCHOOL CLOTHES Children seem to lose everything, from socks to shoes and sports kit. Storage of specific items in dedicated drawers is invaluable to prevent last minute panics at breakfast time. A short rail for hanging shirts, uniform trousers, or skirts is useful. A pretty chest or cupboard may encourage a child to use the storage more.

LEISURE CLOTHES As long as the school clothes are catered for, elder children can be responsible for their own choice of clothes to wear out of school. If you provide them with space to keep them in, they can organize this by themselves. Hanging storage is not usually necessary.

SPECIAL CONSIDERATIONS Babies need a disproportionate amount of storage space. Most clothes can be kept in drawers; lace or silk gowns should be wrapped in tissue paper in a sealed box or bag.

Sharing

WORK CLOTHES Sharers are often students, and work clothes for them are the clothes they wear all day at college or at home. Hanging storage takes up little space, but if there is no room for a wardrobe perhaps a garment rail on castors could be shared by a number of people.

LEISURE CLOTHES Jackets and pretty blouses can be hung on a rail, but little strappy tops can be rolled up in drawers if necessary, along with underwear. It is useful if each person can have one personal chest of drawers.

SPECIAL CONSIDERATIONS Most people have at least three pairs of shoes. They are awkward shapes and, like socks, one of a pair can get lost, so some form of specific shoe storage can really be helpful. There are lots of ideas on the market, from hanging pouches to three-tiered metal racks.

CROSS REFER TO

● Anti-hoarding and
de-cluttering pp.32–3
● Bedroom pp.84–5
● Everyday storage pp.98–9
● Long-term storage pp.104–5

Right A young person's room has to accommodate dozens of interests and activities. By providing flexible storage and a desk space you at least create the means to organize the space to some degree.

Homeworker/student

Working at home takes a lot of discipline. There are always distractions and clashes of priorities. Early on in your home planning you should decide where your work space will be. If you work full time from home you will want to set up as professional a space as possible. If you can spare a room to act as a separate office, that will enable you to work without interruption and will probably be the most satisfactory answer. Your desk or workstation will be the hub of your office. As you are likely to spend a large part of the day in your office, try to make it as congenial as you can. Plan for your ideal—you can always (and will probably have to) pare it down later to suit the actual circumstances, but a lot can be achieved with good planning. The enormous mahogany executive desk of your imagination can be translated into a similar idea but with smaller proportions.

For a student a dedicated room for studying is an unlikely luxury, but you can still create a very efficient work corner in any room using a modern desking system. These can be varied and versatile, with shelves and drawers incorporated, and are often on castors—offering scope for working in a very small dual-purpose room, where you simply pull out your desk to work.

> " Early on in your home planning you should decide where your work space will be. Your desk or workstation will be the hub of your office. As you will spend a large part of the day there, try to make it as congenial as you can. "

Solo Living

SPACE Single occupancy will give you the luxury of being able to place essential equipment, such as your printer, telephone, and stationery where you can reach it easily from your desk.
STYLE Choose a style that will fit in with the general décor of your home. Wood, plywood, MDF, and furniture not designed primarily for office use can all fit in well with a traditional style of home, and there are plenty of modern desking systems that will go with a Minimalist style.
FURNITURE A fold-away work space can be a neat way to conceal your work space. One person is more likely to be able to keep such a space neat enough to put away after work. This can be invaluable in a dual-purpose room in a small flat.

Couples

SPACE Do clearly define the separate areas when sharing office space. Shared equipment should be placed between the two desks, where it can easily be reached by either person. Compact furniture is essential if two people are going to fit comfortably into a small space. Chairs should have narrow seats with no arm rests and desks should be chosen to fit the area (particularly in corners), so no space is wasted.
STYLE Two people working together will create more clutter than just one, so a Minimalist, sleek, simple style will make the space seem less cluttered.
FURNITURE It may be better to choose a modular desk system with an extension for the second person, than to have two completely separate desks.

Family

SPACE Where several members of a family with different interests are sharing a computer/desk space, this must be simple and flexible with as diverse a range of storage and as much work surface as possible.
STYLE A family workstation may be situated in the living room so it should be cheerful and simple, and co-ordinate with the general style of the room. There should be plenty of storage for DVDs, CDs, and computer games. Many families find a notice board invaluable.
FURNITURE If children spend much time on a shared computer, it's worth getting a good, supportive chair. A height-adjustable chair should fit all the family, as a chair at the right height will help to prevent repetitive strain injury (RSI).

Sharing

SPACE Personal space is often scarce in student accommodation. You might want a purpose-designed work station but instead have to share a large table in the living room. Even the smallest table and chair in a corner of a bedroom is worth organizing if you can.
STYLE An ad hoc style may well match the style of the furnishing shared by a number of people. Bright colors can lift the spirits in a very basic interior and make study seem slightly less of a chore.
FURNITURE Second-hand office furniture can be a good answer to finding affordable desks, chairs, and shelves. Spray paint will brighten it up.

CROSS REFER TO

● Eating pp.18–19 ● Bathing pp.20–1
● Sleeping pp.22–3 ● Anti-hoarding and de-cluttering pp.32–3 ● Tiny spaces pp.46–7 ● Landings and box rooms pp.56–7 ● Attics and basements pp.58–9 ● Work space pp.76–9 ● Everyday storage p.101

Assessing the space

Antihoarding and decluttering

If you can't start with a completely empty room then at least you can rationalize the space by decluttering, which will give you a slightly blanker page to work with. The first rule when considering the space in your home is to list everything you own, from the largest upholstered armchair down to the smallest paper clip, so you can be sure to find a home for everything. However, before you begin, throw half of it out. Far from being difficult this should be hugely satisfying, leaving your home feeling larger, less cluttered, and with far greater potential. Arm yourself with several big refuse bags and ruthlessly cast out everything you don't need.

Below right Having decluttered, give reward yourself with some well-divided storage, such as this floor-to-ceiling arrangement in which cubby holes, baskets, drawers, and hangers encourage things to be put in their place.

Below Decluttering is an ongoing exercise for most people, and the owner of this friendly, comfortable, and intriguing room will have to keep a close eye on the state of his/her belongings.

THROW OUT:

- Anything you haven't worn or used within the last year.
- Anything you are clinging on to purely out of nostalgia.
- Anything you think "might come in useful" (it won't, because you won't be able to find it when you need it anyway).
- Everything you've grown out of.
- Everything broken or worn out, including children's toys.
- Beloved but smelly sneakers.
- All out-of-date medicines (but take them to the pharmacist, don't pour them down the drain).
- Out-of-date brochures, takeout menus, newspapers, and magazines.

WHERE TO TAKE IT

Most local authorities now have collections for nonfood refuse and a recycling center where you can take your cast-offs. They may even accept some items of furniture. Charity shops will be grateful for clean clothes in reasonable condition—a sensible way of recycling. Toys and books in good condition may be welcomed by a local hospital or playgroup. Always phone first.

ACTION PLAN

Don't kid yourself you can get rid of clutter in a single afternoon. Allow yourself at least a week to get through your home, and longer if you are at work during the day. Go through it room by room. Just look into one kitchen drawer with decluttering eyes and you will begin to see the scale of the

problem, from pizza leaflets to elastic bands, ancient vitamin pills to cut flower reviver packets—all the things you've swept in there out of sight of sudden visitors. Chuck it all out.

When you get to your essential household filing system, whether it's neatly categorized or jumbled up in drawers, go through the papers carefully before throwing anything away. Amid the chaos important things such as birth certificates and passports are liable to get thrown away by mistake.

When you've finished, remember the rule "One In, One Out"—whenever you buy something new, get rid of something old.

KITCHEN/DINING ROOM

- Throw out broken pens, take-away menus, out-of-date competition and lottery entries, and grocery coupons and vouchers.

- Throw out all redundant kitchen tools, gizmos, and gadgets—even the expensive ones if you don't use them.

- Buy a cutlery divider to fit into a kitchen drawer—a surprising space-saver.

- Throw away at least half the carrier bags you've acquired. Keep the rest in a bag hanging on a hook or get a bag dispenser.

- Throw out all bottles and jars with only dregs in the bottom.

- Throw out anything cracked or chipped.

- Don't keep two sets of china, one for everyday and one for special occasions. Just choose one set that you really like.

LIVING ROOM/OFFICE

- Throw out all half-used candles—are you really going to make new candles with them?

- Throw out cheap objets d'art; they may seem significant but you'll soon forget them.

- Give all paperback books you won't want to read again to a charity shop.

- Throw out all video tapes, CDs, and DVDs that are damaged or you won't use again.

- Throw out cushions that are past their best.

- Throw out chairs that are too large or never get sat in.

- Shred then throw out all out-of-date paperwork (but remember that tax-related business records may have to be kept for up to seven years.)

BATHROOM

- Clear out the medicine chest or wherever old medicines happen to be lurking. Out-of-date medicines should be taken back to a pharmacist for disposal or sealed in a plastic bag and put into the refuse. Don't pour them down the drain.

- Throw out all old soaps, bath and shower products, shampoos, and other toiletries.

- Throw out worn towels, face cloths, loofahs, and sponges that have become slimy.

CHILDREN'S ROOMS

- All broken toys and torn books should go, but do remember to check with the child first. Just before a birthday is a good time.

- Outgrown clothes should be passed on to friends or taken to a charity shop.

- Old buggies may be fun to play with but eventually should be passed on.

CLOTHES

- Lonely single socks must go. If the other one turns up, send it after the first—socks are cheap to replace. Throw away laddered nylons, holey underwear, and baggy bras.

- Throw away faded T-shirts.

- Throw away anything you've grown out of.

- Throw out anything unworn in the last year.

Measuring and documenting

The floor plan you devise should be easy to understand, so include the basic outline of the room with the actual measurements written on it. What you want to show is the floor space, doors and windows, pipe and electric wiring runs, and how things are arranged. Getting the measurements right is crucial.

Decide on the scale of your drawing. Remember whether you've chosen meters or feet to work in, and stick to what you've chosen. Don't aim for perfection. A fairly rough sketch is all you need as long as the measurements are correct. First get the dimensions right and draw the space as you find it. Then make several copies of the drawing and use it as a basis for working out how you want to change it. You can make as many drawings as you like and may do several before you begin to find the right answer.

When actually creating your plan, don't place furniture where it will get in the way of spaces needed to open doors and windows, or to pull out chairs for sitting. If furniture has drawers or doors that need space to open, make sure there is room to do this. Mark the flow of movement through a room and check that your placing of furniture does not interrupt this flow.

> " Make copies of the drawing and use it as a basis for working out what to change ... you may do several before you find the right answer. "

YOU WILL NEED

- A good retractable tape measure ☐
- A pad of squared (graph) paper ☐
- A pad of tracing paper ☐
- Pencils and an eraser ☐
- Colored felt-tip pens to mark pipes and wiring ☐
- A notebook ☐
- Masking tape ☐
- Ruler ☐
- Possibly a second person to help hold the tape measure ☐

SOME GUIDELINES WHEN MEASURING

- Always draw in pencil.

- If using a scale rule, a scale of 1:50 should be suitable for a plan of a room 27 x 17ft (8.2 x 5m) to fit on a sheet of paper. Alternatively you could decide that 10ft 7in (1sq m) will be equal to, say, 3sq in (2sq cm) on an ordinary ruler.

- Fix the tracing paper to the graph paper with masking tape, using the cardboard backing of the pad or a piece of board to hold it firm.

- Measure the walls and draw the overall width and length of the room, starting from the corner to the left of the entrance door.

- Measure the projections and openings, chimney breasts, doors and windows,

skirting boards and radiators, fireplaces (even if bricked up), alcoves, and other architectural features.

- Mark the space required to open doors and windows.

- Mark existing electric and phone sockets, and pipe and electric wiring runs.

- Mark where the floors change level.

- Write the measurements on your drawing as a check against inaccuracies, and give information about details.

- For appliances transcribe the dimensions from catalogs or measure the actual appliance and divide by 20 to give a 1:20 scale.

Drawing a plan

Most homeowners don't know the dimensions of their rooms and base their decisions on an imagined, idealized size and shape. However, it is invaluable to know exactly what you are dealing with when choosing furniture. Estate agents will give measurements but these are not always accurate, so it's safer to check them for yourself. Be aware that narrow staircases may not allow a double bed or a three-seater sofa to go up them.

If either dimension of a room is less than 10ft (3m), designers classify it as small. If either dimension is greater than 30ft (9m), that is considered large, and the best use would be to divide it into smaller areas. This is ideal if you want it to double up as a work room or a dining room.

A plan is invaluable when working out how furniture, cupboards, and appliances will fit in to create practical, pleasant spaces. If you are designing the arrangement of a small bedroom there may be little leeway or room for manoeuvre. By the time you've fitted in a bed and some clothes storage, plus a small table, you may think there will be no room for anything else. However, If you work things out to scale on graph paper you may find you can organize things differently (without having to move heavy furniture around).

A plan is even more important when designing a complicated kitchen. Remember that you need space to be able to bend down to get things out of low cupboards, that chairs have to be pulled away from the table or desk so you can sit down, and that appliances have doors that can be awkward to open in a small space.

If your plan leads you to think you'd like to alter the space itself, to pull down a wall to make a larger space out of two small ones or change the siting of a bathroom, you will need permission from the relevant authority. There are international regulations to ensure that a so-called "habitable" room has natural light and adequate ventilation. Rooms without windows can only be used as non-habitable (i.e., storage, bathroom, or service areas). And you cannot add a window if it will look out onto an adjoining home. If you intend to do any major work, seek professional advice first.

KITCHEN/LIVING ROOM

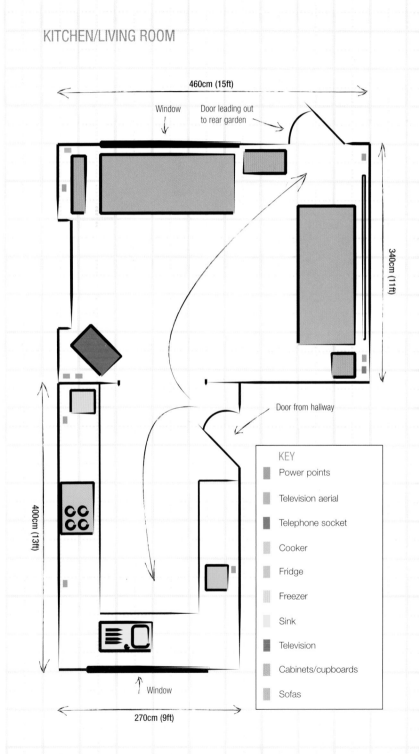

460cm (15ft)

Window

Door leading out to rear garden

340cm (11ft)

Door from hallway

400cm (13ft)

270cm (9ft)

Window

KEY

- Power points
- Television aerial
- Telephone socket
- Cooker
- Fridge
- Freezer
- Sink
- Television
- Cabinets/cupboards
- Sofas

Studio apartments

Fitting your whole life into one room needs serious planning. You may have to cook, eat, sleep, entertain, and work in the one space, and the aim is to create a multi-purpose area that is friendly, comfortable, and a pleasure to come home to. This is easier said than done, and a scale floorplan can really be helpful to work out what size of furniture you can include and how to arrange it. Divide the room into separate activity areas, with a permanent room divider in the form of floor-to-ceiling shelving. You could differentiate between a working/living area and a separate cooking/eating area that way. The shelves will give glimpses of the room beyond, and let in a certain amount of light to create an impression of spaciousness.

In a very small room a permanent divider is likely to create two rather claustrophobic areas, so it might be better to have a folding screen to act as a visual barrier. In a larger room you can divide the areas by arranging furniture in different groupings, but a large space with no divisions can become rather tedious and it's probably a better idea to introduce some tall storage anyway. The secret is to have an attractive, coordinated, but extremely simple design, with only the basic essentials, and to make the furniture work really hard, doubling up in use wherever possible. In a restricted space, opt for the smallest of everything so the room is not dominated by the furniture.

CHECKLIST

WHAT YOU NEED

- Somewhere to sleep ☐
- Somewhere to sit ☐
- Somewhere to cook/eat ☐
- Somewhere to work ☐
- Somewhere to entertain ☐
- Enough storage ☐

Above This large, rather low space is kept deliberately uncluttered, giving a feeling of restfulness and relaxation. The emphasis is on natural materials such as wood, leather, and wool.

Right A tall warehouse development makes good use of the room height with a mezzanine-level bedroom. The simple staircase, furniture, and monochrome finish unifies the space.

Sleeping

PLANNING The bed is probably the largest item of furniture you will need, so early on decide what sort of bed to choose and where to put it. You can save space effectively by doubling up your bed as seating. Try before you buy—the mattress mustn't sag when you sit on the edge if you're going to use it as seating as well.

MEASUREMENTS If you want to place the bed in the center of the room, measure carefully to be sure it doesn't interrupt the flow of movement through the space. Remember, too, that chairs always take up more space when being used so allow for that when planning.

PRACTICAL IDEA A small divan or futon can be freestanding and take its place as the center of a seating area. Your measurements will tell you which will work best.

Cooking

PLANNING Plan for the minimum amount of cooking and kitchen storage space. Whittle your equipment down to the absolute basics—the tiniest sink and minimum cutlery and china. Then allow for just enough storage space for these items and no more.

MEASUREMENTS A space 6ft 6in (2m) wide is the narrowest you can hope to use as a kitchen, so this will decide whether you can add a room divider/breakfast bar. You can create the impression of width by fixing open shelves rather than cupboard doors (which seem to bring the walls forward).

PRACTICAL IDEA Instead of a conventional oven and stovetop perhaps make do with one or two small appliances, such as a microwave or a plug-in grill. The space saved by foregoing the built-in cooker should provide enough worktop space for these, plus extra storage underneath.

Working

PLANNING Your sketch plan is vital here. You can plan for your work desk to double up as a dining table, or decide to eat informally in front of the TV. You can then have a workstation that is dedicated entirely to your work and carries all its own storage compartments.

MEASUREMENTS Refer to your sketch plan to find out whether you can fit your work area into one corner of the room. There are plenty of purpose-designed corner desk units that may make use of an otherwise dead space. Check the measurements of the desk units you have in mind, as well as the area of the room.

PRACTICAL IDEA Castors are a true blessing in a multi-purpose room. Your work station can be pulled away from the wall when you need it; modern beds are often designed with castors, making it possible to swivel them and adjust their position.

Above Successful Minimalist living requires few belongings and a lot of discipline. This Japanese-influenced room uses a moveable *shoji* screen divider, a futon as both bed and seating, and a low table for reading.

> " The aim is to create a multi-purpose space that is friendly, comfortable, and a pleasure to come home to. "

Dual-purpose rooms

There are several activities that lend themselves to sharing a space. For example, a kitchen/diner makes good sense in that you don't have to carry the food from one room to another, while things like cutlery and china can share storage space. Equally, a work area can often be fitted into a bedroom or a living room. In such cases, the work area can often share furniture and certainly the furniture style with the bed or living-room furniture. Designing such dual-purpose spaces does require very careful planning and assessment so a sketch plan is a useful tool.

In a small space, if you can make furniture multitask you will need fewer pieces. However, multi-task often sounds more convenient than it actually is. If you are working, you will not necessarily want to clear the desk every time in order to eat, whereas a comfortable upright chair may well be used for both dining or work. Bed sizes vary enormously in both width and height, so check what's available before trying to fit a bed into a space. Consider altering the layout of radiators, or of installing skirting radiators, to allow for a convenient arrangement of furniture.

CHECKLIST

WHAT YOU NEED

- Kitchen/dining ☐
- Kitchen/office ☐
- Office/dining ☐
- Bedroom/office ☐
- Living room/office ☐
- Living room/dining ☐

Left Here cooking and eating are closely integrated with storage for both activities. A series of fitted cupboards and open shelves acts as kitchen units and dining room "dresser," with a table large enough to seat four people.

Kitchen/dining

PLANNING You could arrange the cooking area in a corner of the room where the worktops and services create an L shape along two walls, leaving a wide enough area to take a small round table. Make sure there is adequate seating space where the process of cooking won't disturb the diners.

MEASUREMENTS Allow 26in (65cm) for bending down to open the oven door without bumping into anything.

PRACTICAL IDEA It should be possible to arrange storage that can be reached from both areas, so you can store things such as cutlery and plates that are common to both.

Office/dining

PLANNING A practical dual purpose combination is the dining room/office as the room is probably only used for dining occasionally, allowing the rest of the time for uninterrupted work. The style of the furniture should be compatible, otherwise the office element may dominate, making dining somewhat uncomfortable.

MEASUREMENTS Allow at least 28in (70cm) for your chair when sitting at the desk or table. Make sure you can fit in enough storage for both uses of the room.

PRACTICAL IDEA A small trolley on castors may be a convenient way of temporarily storing ongoing work without needing to disturb it.

Bedroom/office

PLANNING In the bedroom you want to be sure the work element is discreet and not going to be a constant distraction when you are trying to go to sleep at night. A physical room divider, such as wide wall-to-ceiling shelves, can double up as office shelving on one side and bedroom storage on the other.

MEASUREMENTS Measure carefully and work out whether there is room for a storage/room divider or if this will create two claustrophobic spaces.

PRACTICAL IDEA Failing an actual room divider, consider concealing the work area with an attractive panelled folding screen. A Japanese-style *shoji* screen of transparent paper has the advantage of letting light through, adding to the sense of space.

Above In this very small space a built-in bed is well integrated, with its own neatly incorporated desk space and pin board. An adjustable desklight can be focused towards the bed or the desk.

Top A dining room can double as an office but install plenty of storage to clear away work in progress and ensure the office equipment does not dominate.

It is possible to divide up a space so that you create two separate areas but still allow a through view, which makes the space seem larger. Leaving the division "open" in some way allows more light through and gives a sense of perspective. This is a particularly useful strategy in long narrow rooms as the division provides each area with better proportions but the openness creates the impression of one large space. Such a division could be built-in or in the form of a portable screen; either way it should look aesthetically pleasing in its own right. It could also include storage or somewhere to sit, or it could be purely decorative.

Right A decorative screen provides a stylish division between the bedroom and bathroom areas. The simplicity of the furniture and the use of white give a feeling of unity and space to the room.

Below This kitchen breaks up what was a long, narrow room while still allowing an overall feeling of space.

Creating alcoves

PLANNING If two rooms have been knocked into one, you can create an alcove by building a wide arch between the rooms, using medium density fibreboard (MDF). This is a stable material that won't warp or crack. Use standard ¾in (19mm) MDF sheeting for good rigidity.

MEASUREMENTS The depth of an arch could be as much as 21½in (550mm), which would house a small fridge or freezer and a wine rack. A shallower depth would create bookshelves.

PRACTICAL IDEA In a bedroom you could cover alcoves with louvred doors, thus creating useful cupboards rather than open shelves.

Creating other pocket spaces

PLANNING You might be able to plan two narrow cupboards at either end of the wall in an interior lobby, which will create one alcove between them. This space could be used for a small desk or dressing table.

MEASUREMENTS Measure the space between the end of the bath and the wall and see if it is adequate for a purpose-built space for housing the washing machine and dryer. Check with the local authority that this conforms to safety regulations.

PRACTICAL IDEA Build a platform above a bedroom door to provide invaluable storage.

Right A narrow window seat forms a comfortable seating area, with informal striped cushions that mirror the blinds.

Understairs—open

The space under the stairs in a home is nearly always underused. It may take different forms, depending on which way the stairs run and how wide or narrow they are. In small, traditional town houses the stairs often lead directly from the hall to the first floor and can be narrow and pokey. The conventional staircase is usually boxed in by a non-load-bearing wall and takes up a large part of the ground floor space. Removing this wall to reveal the space under the stairs can create a feeling of greater spaciousness but also provide a useful addition to the living or storage space. Some more recently built homes may already have open staircases, and the space underneath them should certainly not be wasted.

Such space offers good opportunities for housing music equipment, a small work area, a place for telephoning, or even a spare bed. Your measurements will tell you how useful this space can be for comfortable seating, or whether simply to organize it as storage. You could consider replacing a conventional staircase with a spiral one but, although elegant, they actually take up more space and it's impossible to get large pieces of furniture up or down.

CHECKLIST
POSSIBLE USES
• Shelves ☐
• Hanging storage ☐
• Seating ☐
• Picture display ☐
• Blanket chest ☐
• Small desk ☐
• Fridge/freezer ☐
• Piano/keyboard ☐

Above This basic pine staircase has no banister so the small pictures placed on the risers are seen to good advantage, while the fitted wine rack underneath can house a complete cellar of coveted wines.

Simple storage

PLANNING If the stairs are narrow, a series of tapered shelves may be the most versatile form of storage. They must be easy to get at without banging your head, so the lower section might be better with pull-out storage boxes on castors.

MEASUREMENTS Stairs vary in width, length, and in steepness so measure all the dimensions and the angles when working out the width and length of the shelves and then check on your sketch plan that everything will fit.

PRACTICAL IDEA Rather than have a full wall of shelves, leave a gap between them where you can hang a painting, print, or a series of photographs. This helps to integrate the understairs section of the room with the main area.

Seating area

PLANNING If the room is tall, the stairs will probably leave a generous space under the top section to make a congenial seating area with comfortable settees and chairs.

MEASUREMENTS Dimensions are important here. Don't try to get a two-seater sofa in a space only suitable for a small stool. Cut out to-scale shapes for any furniture you want to include and try them out on your plan.

PRACTICAL IDEA If the stairs are narrow and low, use the space for a narrow desk or table, with an upright chair facing the wall rather than trying to incorporate it as part of the main living area.

Unconventional

PLANNING Think of your own circumstances and see if any of the things you own but find hard to place will fit under the stairs. Remember, if you've opened up the space you will want something that is decorative and good looking, not a large bag of sports equipment.

MEASUREMENTS If you are thinking of a space for a refrigerator/freezer, remember that dimensions for staircases vary so measure the height, depth, and width required for the particular appliance you have chosen. If it won't fit by a centimeter or so, see if you can find a slightly smaller model.

PRACTICAL IDEA A musical instrument such as a piano or electric keyboard, which are bulky and large and often hard to find room for, might fit well under the staircase.

Left Space under the stairs is often wasted, but here it has been deliberately used as a display area with a traditional kitchen table surrounded by objects, baskets, and books that admirably complement its style.

Below This modern conversion has successfully incorporated a seating/sleeping area under the stairs that relates well with the rest of the room, including the recessed cube storage and inset stair lights.

Understairs—enclosed

Sometimes you may prefer to keep the space under the stairs enclosed, leaving room for storage you wish hidden from view. In order to do this you would have to remove the existing wall and fit cupboard doors. These could either be paneled or plain, and could be decorated to match the rest of the room or painted in a contrasting color. If the stairs are in a hallway, the space underneath them can be usefully used as hanging storage for coats. Or you could create a whole bank of tall cupboards and drawers carefully designed to hold specific objects, with the tall cupboards for the taller objects, gradually diminishing in height as the stairs descend. This is a practical and efficient way of storing a large number of objects. Another possibility is to have half the space concealed by doors and the lower space fitted with open shelves to house a sound center, including speakers and storage for CDs.

In larger spaces, such as those found under the main steps to a traditional townhouse, you might be able to squeeze in a tiny shower cubicle or even a miniscule bath—the kind you sit up in. There are baths in all sorts of sizes and variations in shape so it's worth searching around for the smallest you can find. If not a bath, then you might want to install your washing machine under the stairs. For anything involving plumbing, get a professional designer or plumbing specialist to advise. There are regulations covering plumbing that must be followed.

CHECKLIST
POSSIBLE USES
• Bank of cupboards and drawers ☐
• Coat storage ☐
• Concealed shelving ☐
• Broom cupboard ☐
• Toys ☐
• Gardening equipment ☐
• Sewing equipment ☐
• Dirty laundry ☐
• Linen cupboard ☐
• Shower ☐
• Bath ☐

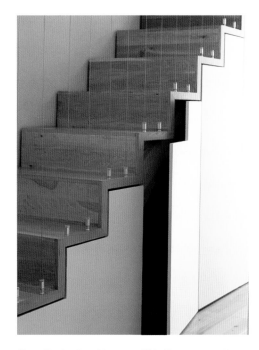

Above Fitted cupboard doors under the stairs conceal separate pockets of storage, creating a modern, unfussy look with its own secret practicality. The divisions of the space make organization of the storage easier.

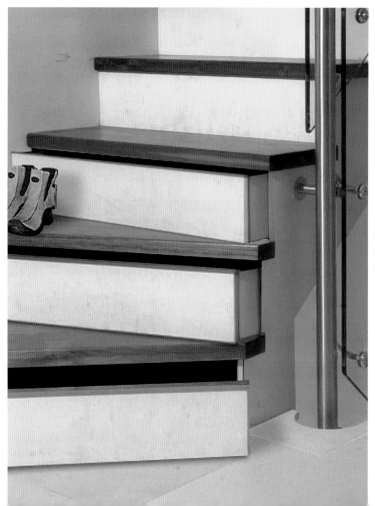

Right The drawers in this specially designed curved staircase take the place of conventional risers, providing the perfect storage space for shoes (often difficult objects to store) and complementing the modern, minimal look.

Attic

PLANNING Windows should be an integral part of your planning. Rooflights bring in clear, bright daylight. They can easily be fitted into a roof; place them high for privacy, lower for a view.

MEASUREMENTS You can gain around 19.3sq ft (1.8sq m) of floor space by pushing a bed back under the angle of the roof during the day—ideal in a child's room where floor space is important for playing. A bed on castors makes this easier.

PRACTICAL IDEA Build an extra wall in front of the A-shaped wall at the end, creating a walk-in cupboard for clothes and other large items.

Basement

PLANNING Deep basements tend to be cave-like and difficult to bring light into. You can divide up the space by building interior walls, leaving the front and the back as habitable rooms, and the central part for windowless storage or perhaps a bathroom.

MEASUREMENTS On your plan, find out if you can fit a double-glazed sliding patio door in place of the existing exterior wall. If you can create a small patio outside you will bring more light into the room.

PRACTICAL IDEA Line the back wall of the room with mirror panels to enhance the light and reflect the garden.

Converting

PLANNING Moving up into the roof or removing walls in a basement to create one large space will be expensive. You may prefer to make the most of the space as it exists. However, if you are considering a conversion remember that many houses are not strong enough to support any extra building upwards, and the cost of strengthening may make such a plan simply unviable.

MEASUREMENTS To be classed as a living room or bedroom (habitable space) the height must be at least 7ft 6in (2.25m) over at least half of the existing space. Also, such rooms will probably need a permanent staircase, not a ladder, and one that is not too narrow and not too steep. If you can't convert, rationalize the space and design it for storage instead.

PRACTICAL IDEA You can sometimes overcome the height regulations by building a mezzanine floor or gallery. Get professional advice for this.

Below left A table and shelving are well-placed under a roof light in the lower part of this converted attic. The height in the centre has been used to create a platform for sleeping.

Below This cavern-like basement is a practical and generous workroom. White walls give a sense of space.

THIS CHAPTER SUGGESTS many ways of using the interior spaces of your home, with various designs and arrangements of free-standing and built-in furniture. Once you have taken a good look at your own lifestyle and sketched out the different areas in your home you will be quite familiar with the spaces, know where the awkward corners are, where there is potential, and which particular ideas will not work.

Now you can begin the practical adventure of furnishing. You will probably have decided what the general arrangement is going to be, how the flow of movement should work, and what sort of furniture you want. This includes items you already own and intend to keep. Using existing furniture is cheaper than buying everything new, but if a piece is large, bulky, or in a certain style, hanging on to it may mean sacrificing some good space-saving ideas. Make the most of what's already there: a kitchen table can act as a preparation area as well as a dining table. And kitchen cupboards or wardrobes can be made to hold twice as much if they are fitted with drawers, wire baskets, hooks, and other sorting devices.

Using the space

Creating a home

You will want your home to reflect your interests and your own tastes. As far as style is concerned, you may want to create an informal, eclectic scheme with no particular historical connections. An informal style implies versatility and a relaxed attitude, not complete chaos. It means you can put together different elements to create a very personal space, with furniture chosen for its comfort and practicality rather than purely for its looks. When deciding what sort of style to choose, work with the character of your home's architecture rather than against it. For example, if you live in a modern apartment whose rooms are mainly square and unadorned you could choose a Minimalist style very successfully, but a grand Louis XVII style with ceiling mouldings and deep chandeliers would be difficult to achieve.

Whatever style or nonstyle you choose, proportion and scale are important. You might get a large settee into a small room but it will dwarf any other furniture and you could seat people just as comfortably on more pieces of smaller furniture. Equally, it's only worth introducing an enormous, family-sized refrigerator/freezer in a kitchen if you can position it right at the end of a run of units so it doesn't dominate the whole room.

Keep your eyes open for ingenious ideas for arranging furniture. Stores, other people's homes, and glossy magazines are all full of suggestions. There's a huge variety of designs of furniture and storage items in a wide range of materials, and somewhere out there is the very thing you need. Above all, keep checking back to your measurements and sketches—they are vital to make sure that what you've set your heart on is actually what you need. They will prevent you from sudden impulse buys that won't fit anywhere.

Right This room has been thoughtfully organized to bring in lots of light, with glass doors extending the space onto the patio. The cooking is confined to one wall and freestanding furniture makes it as much living room as kitchen.

> "You can put together different elements to create a very personal space, with furniture chosen for its comfort and practicality rather than purely for its looks. Whatever style or nonstyle you choose, proportion and scale are important. "

CHECKLIST

WHAT TO REMEMBER

- List all your belongings ☐
- Check size of appliances ☐
- Check size of furniture ☐
- Check size of spaces ☐
- Check width of stairs ☐
- Check width of doors ☐
- Ensure plenty of work surfaces ☐
- Use available height ☐
- Use pockets of space ☐
- Ensure plenty of storage ☐
- Purpose-design your storage ☐
- Allow space for future acquisitions ☐

Living and entertaining

ARRANGING THE SEATING AREA

The most important aspect of a living room is the main seating area. This is where you will watch TV, listen to music, entertain visitors, chat, and often eat as well. It's tempting to get an enormous settee and a couple of easy chairs to flop into, but this is seldom as comfortable as it sounds. Three people rarely sit on a three-piece sofa together—three is not a companionable number—so a large part of its size will be wasted. Smaller, perhaps modular seating that can be re-arranged, moved, or even turned to face the other way can be just as welcoming and far more flexible. Seating must be comfortable—not too short in the seat and not too difficult to get in and out of. You will need a surface nearby on which to put glasses, nibbles, or telephones.

Seating is usually arranged to face some kind of focal point, often the television. Another effective and popular focal point is a traditional fireplace; woodburning stoves or decorative modern electric fires can be equally attractive. More unusually you could choose a striking textile hanging or a sculpture as your focal point, with the television set slightly to one side so as not to dominate the room.

WHAT TO CONSIDER

- Can you divide the room by a bookcase, accessible from either side? ☐
- Can you use a chair that can double as bedroom furniture when you have a guest? ☐
- Can your desk double up as a dressing table? ☐
- Have you got room for a slim cupboard where office equipment can be neatly hidden away when not in use? ☐

Recessed ceiling lights give good illumination without glare.

A short, room-high partition fitted at one end of the room gives alcove space for shelves.

The same partition can create a separate office or reading space beyond.

Children's chairs should be simple and sturdy with a wide base, but can still look stylish.

Dining chairs should fit snugly under the table when not in use.

SEATING

- Avoid huge, heavy furniture that is difficult to move and takes up too much space.

- Avoid three-piece suites, which are inflexible and greedy of space.

- Modular seating is versatile and available in many configurations.

- A long, low coffee table can make a good (and practical) focal point in front of seating.

- A chaise longue or a day bed may be more elegant and versatile than a settee.

- Nesting tables provide individual "parking" spaces for cups and mugs.

- Large cushions create good backrests for divan seating or can be used on the floor.

- Experiment with placement: two two-seater sofas at right angles, or an arrangement of seating at a slight angle to the focal point.

- Create separate zones so that different parts of the room can be used separately.

FIREPLACES

- Traditional 18th- and 19th-century fireplaces are often highly decorative, with generous mantelshelves and fine proportions. They make fantastic centrepieces even if not actually in use.

- A gas or electric fireplace with a modern surround can complement a minimalist interior.

- Woodburning stoves are a good way to heat a room, and some heat the water too. Available in a range of styles, from traditional to ultramodern, they make attractive focal points.

- A modern, stark white, simple surround with the simplest grate or no fire at all is superbly suited to a Modernist interior. Fill the center with a large vase of flowers or foliage, or with a modern sculpture.

- A low, wide fireplace will look good in a room with a low ceiling, where it can reflect the shape of the room.

OTHER FOCAL POINTS

- A substantial, low coffee table might have drawers or a shelf for books, with a flower arrangement or display of objects on top.

- If yours is a tall apartment with a picture window and a grand view, perhaps of sea or countryside, place the seating facing the window to make the view the focal point.

- A textile can make a visually stimulating and colorful point of interest. A patchwork, an embroidered picture, or a woven kilim can all be warm and interesting. Hang it from a curtain rod or stretch it over wooden battens.

- If your TV is the focal point, consider a flat screen fixed to the wall to save space.

- Instead of the usual coffee table you could have an upholstered ottoman—good as a footstool or table—between two facing areas of seating. Cover it with a substantial fabric, such as an old Middle Eastern kilim rug or a dhurrie from India.

A lowered ceiling can make a tall room more snug and allow space for recessed lighting.

A window with a view can be framed by curtains but use sheer fabrics that won't cut out the light.

A tall mirror next to the window reflects the room, making it seem twice its length.

Padded dining chairs in a simple check fabric soften the lines of the kitchen storage.

Plain white shelves house glasses and china, making the most of their decorative qualities.

Co-ordinated cupboards and appliances give this informal kitchen/dining room a comfortable, unified look.

CROSS REFER TO

● Eating pp.18–19
● Entertaining pp.28–9
● Understairs—open pp.50–1 ● Halls and corridors pp.54–5 ● Cooking pp.68–71 ● Eating pp.72–5
● Use of lighting pp.120–26
● Use of colour pp.128–31
● Screens and dividers pp.136–7

SPACE-SAVING FURNITURE AND IDEAS FOR DISPLAY

The living room probably has more potential functions than any other room in the house. It may have to act as the dining room; it may be the place for putting guests up overnight; it may house your desk and computer area; or it may have young children playing there during the day. Choosing and sticking to a particular style will help to co-ordinate these multiple functions. In general, the simpler the room is the better it will look.

It makes sense to search out well-designed, space-saving furniture. This may mean furniture that can be used for different purposes, or neatly designed pieces that will fit into a small space while still looking good and being practical and comfortable to use. It will certainly mean discarding any idea of a lavishly upholstered three- or four-piece suite in favor of a generous two-seater or a compact modular range that can be arranged to suit your needs. If you want to incorporate a dining area in the room, choose chairs that can be used in any part of the room and moved around as necessary. Extra folding chairs can be kept elsewhere until needed.

Essentially the style choice for a room is between formal and informal. Formality is associated with symmetry and the disciplined placing of furniture. Informality indicates a feeling of comfort and relaxation and a somewhat haphazard approach, using individual pieces rather than "suites." Whatever you choose, whether formal or informal, a well-designed room should not feel too busy.

Below left This simple chunky style, with its matching seating and basic shelving, can be very comfortable and relaxing. The sturdy, oversized castor wheels allow the small coffee table to be moved.

Below This Minimalist storage system is fixed to the wall, leaving the floor unadorned. The wall-hung TV and hi-tech speakers ensure good viewing.

Right The U-shaped arrangement of these matching sofas in an open-plan environment creates a relaxing living area, clearly separated from the kitchen by a stainless-steel island divider.

"

Whatever you choose, whether formal or informal, a well-designed room should not feel too busy. "

SPACE-SAVING SEATING

- The futon is a form of Japanese bed that originally used to be rolled up and put away during the day. The modern western form of futon mattress (single or double) is available with a base, folding up to become seating during the day.

- In a studio appartment, large cushions can make comfortable backrests against a day bed, or be used on the floor if more visitors turn up.

- The traditional chaise longue can be a good alternative to a settee in a very small room. There are many modern designs from which to choose.

- Modular seating is available in many variations. You can buy as little or as much as you like and use it in numerous configurations.

- Canvas armchairs with bentwood frames are as comfortable as many upholstered armchairs and take up far less space.

SPACE-SAVING TABLES

- A gate-leg table or other folding table can be folded against a wall and opened up when needed, or left fully open and folded only when you need more space.

- An extending table is ideal for a dining area: you can adjust the size according to the number of people who are going to eat.

- A tray-table on wheels provides a good-looking trolley, invaluable for bringing impromptu food and drinks into the room from elsewhere.

- A narrow console table, commonly used in a narrow hallway, can be useful in a small living room that has to fulfil many functions. It can be used as a display space and will be even more useful if it has a shelf beneath the table top.

- Nesting tables are handy for TV meals. There are many to choose from, including traditional designs in wood or modern ones in clear or colored acrylic.

- A card table is an invaluable piece of furniture, with endless uses and the ability to be stored away in a narrow space.

SPACE-SAVING STORAGE IDEAS

- If planning built-in cupboards, make them shallower than normal cupboards so as to take up less space. They can be useful for storing paperback novels, other small books, small objects, CDs, DVDs, and video collections.

- Built-in cupboards can be given glass fronts for displaying decorative objects that will attract attention away from the confines of the room.

- Avoid deep cupboards that take up a lot of space and in which objects can get terminally lost.

- Don't waste the window space. A window seat with shelves or a cupboard underneath can provide both extra seating and storage, and looks particularly good in a tall room.

- It is important to find storage for the many CDs and discs of various kinds that litter most living rooms. If you are incorporating them among bookshelves, make sure the shelf is the right depth to take them or they will look out of place.

- There's a big choice of ready-to-buy storage available so find something that will fit conveniently into your room.

Cooking

ARRANGING THE WORK SEQUENCE

Its complex uses and often constrained space requires the kitchen to be particularly carefully planned. There are some useful guidelines for the layout of an efficient and practical kitchen, no matter how small the space. It's helpful to look at the sequence of events in the cooking process, which consists of storage, food preparation, and cooking.

For storage the refrigerator/freezer is the first consideration. Some things, such as tomatoes or white wine, lose their flavor when over-chilled, so a small, cool cupboard or a larder section in the refrigerator is a good idea. You will need separate storage for tins and jars, dry foods, and fresh fruit and vegetables.

For food preparation you will need work surfaces for chopping, rolling out pastry, mixing, and general preparation, as well as a sink with a drainer.

What you need for the actual cooking will depend on the sort of chef you are. A conventional oven and hob will cook most things, but for some people a microwave is sufficient, or possibly a plug-in grill pan or casserole.

WHAT TO CONSIDER
• Have you enough preparation area? ☐
• Are the cooking facilities (such as ovens) enough, or too much, for your needs? ☐
• Are the interior fitments for cupboards practical and efficient? ☐
• Have you got enough narrow shelves for jars and tins? ☐

The space under the main house stairs has been used to tuck in a worktop and glass shelves.

A stainless-steel cooker gives a professional finish, even in a small space.

A fitted towel rail on a cooker provides a convenient place for tea towels to dry.

A curved sink with curved cupboards takes up less space than one with squared edges.

Choose flooring that is easy to clean, heatproof, and stainproof.

FOOD STORAGE

- Mark on your plan which will be the most convenient way for the cupboard doors to open and make sure, when buying cupboards and the refrigerator, that the doors can open the way you have marked.

- Some foods, such as tomatoes, lose their flavor if they are kept at too low a temperature. If possible, make room for such foods in a cool, airy cupboard.

- Fresh fruit and vegetables should be kept in airy baskets or shelves; tiered shelves help to keep items separate.

- Narrow pull-out storage "drawers," divided by wire compartments, are available in many kitchen designs. These will hold narrow objects, such as herb or spice jars, as well as dry foods like rice and lentils.

- Narrow shelves are useful for storing tins and jars, where they can be easily seen and not lost behind each other.

FOOD PREPARATION AREAS

- A butcher block trolley can be useful as a work surface and doubles up as storage, while having the advantage that you can wheel it around for convenience.

- Position your chopping boards near the sink for easy washing and waste disposal.

- Choice of work surface is important. Wood always looks good, but near the cooker you should add an inset of something heatproof. Other materials include stainless steel, slate, and Corian—a scorch- and stainproof synthetic.

- Sinks are available in many shapes, sizes, and materials. A double sink can be very convenient but, if you lack space, a single sink with a draining board will be fine.

- If you are very short of work surfaces consider installing a half-circle table, hinged to the wall, that you can open up for food preparation and even use for dining.

COOKING

- A section of worktop slightly lower than normal, with the stovetop inset, can be easier to reach than a stovetop at standard height. However, this is not recommended if you have small children.

- A separate stovetop and oven is probably more versatile and easier to fit in than an all-in-one oven.

- In a tiny, one-person kitchen, and for those who don't cook much, it might be better to make do simply with a microwave oven (either built-in or freestanding), with perhaps a plug-in grill as well. There are also a number of versatile, small, table-top cookers worth investigating.

- Ensure the stovetop is not directly under a window, where a draft may fan the flames.

- It is wise to use a combination of fuels. With a gas stovetop and electric oven you won't be stuck if there's a power cut.

During the day the cook has a pleasant view, with no curtains to reduce the light.

A wall downlighter gives an efficient and pleasant light over the sink area.

A small shelf on the wall holds everyday items that can be reached easily.

This traditional fireclay sink has a clean, modern look.

A series of deep drawers next to the cooker can hold bulky items such as saucepans and lids.

The dishwasher next to the sink fits under a low worktop—a good height for chopping.

CROSS REFER TO
- Eating pp. 72–5
- Large appliances pp.92–3
- Kitchen storage pp.106–9
- Use of lighting pp. 122–3

FITTING IT ALL IN

Kitchen cupboards and units are generally made to standard sizes, although other sizes are available in the more expensive designs and may suit you better if you are either taller or shorter than most people. Standard units are cheaper than purpose-built ones and are very varied in their potential and styles. People in wheelchairs should have the kitchen purpose-designed and built since there is less "reach" from a chair. It's common to line the kitchen walls with both base units and head-height cupboards. But if you don't need so many cupboards, you can save both money and space by leaving the wall area for a painting or some other form of storage, such as a long rail with hooks for hanging saucepans.

CHOOSING UNITS FOR THE KITCHEN

- Don't forget to allow for some sort of waste disposal that won't take up lots of floor space. A bin fixed to the inside of a cupboard door and a waste-disposal unit are both convenient.

- Some base units are designed to be fixed onto the wall at the height most convenient to you.

- Some base units are fitted with adjustable legs so you can alter the height as they are installed.

- Make sure the furniture you choose offers right- or left-hand opening doors and that when ordering specify the ones you need.

- Interior fittings exist for any use you like to imagine. Research well and make sure you choose what will best fit into your kitchen and cooking style.

- A corner cupboard can have a "lazy Susan" fitted that rotates so you can get to the objects at the back.

- List the foods, cooking equipment, and other items you keep in the kitchen and work out the minimum number of cupboards needed to store them.

PLACING UNITS

- Make the most of windows by placing the sink, or some other preparation area where you spend some time, underneath.

- Block up any unnecessary doors so that the kitchen doesn't become a throughway, which will be both unsatisfactory and dangerous.

- Work out where to put any radiators; they do not have to interrupt the working area. You might even find a wall space where the radiator could look sculptural or double up as a rail for hand and tea towels.

- Make good use of corners by with specially designed corner units and cupboards.

Left In this tiny space fitted cupboards have left a niche in which to fit the fridge/freezer, so that all the equipment fits into clean lines and yet provides plenty of storage tucked away behind doors.

Above It's worth researching shapes of sinks, such as this curvy one that can be fitted into the end of a small space, with a Corian worktop fitted round it. The purpose-built cupboards include fitted wine racks.

Left This is a very businesslike kitchen, running along just one wall but managing to provide plenty of storage, plenty of work space, and room for one or two luxury items, such as a coffee maker.

- In a very narrow kitchen, avoid deep cupboards at head height whose doors can open to hit you on the head. Or avoid cupboards altogether and install shelves.

PLACING APPLIANCES

- A dishwasher is ideally placed next to the sink, where it can share the plumbing.

- A small single-person dishwasher can sit on the worktop next to the sink.

- Standard refrigerators and freezers are made to fit under standard worktop surfaces. They will need adequate ventilation, which means leaving a space between the back of the appliance and the wall.

- A good arrangement for a stovetop is to place the hotplates or gas burners in a line at the back of the work surface. This is a good safety strategy if there are children around, and the front becomes useful preparation area.

- Sinks come in many shapes and sizes, from single to double to those with a compartment for vegetable peeling.

- Sinks also come in many durable materials, from fireclay to stainless steel or Corian.

- Avoid having too many cupboards as this encourages storage of unnecessary foods and more implements than you need.

Eating

THE FURNITURE

Dining furniture should be attractive but fit neatly into the space you have allotted to it. There are many materials that lend themselves to modern interiors, or for dual-purposes such as eating and working, or doubling up as kitchen/dining tables. And, of course, any table can be transformed by a pretty tablecloth.

Expanding tables are obviously invaluable in small spaces. There are tables with leaves that fold right back along the length to turn into narrow console tables. Others have an extra leaf that can be slotted in, or a leaf that folds down at the end.

Choose chairs carefully. They should be without arms and have narrow backs and seats; otherwise, a table that should be able to seat eight will only take six people.

As for storage, there are innumerable solutions, from tall dressers and traditional armoires to low sideboards and shared storage for dual-purpose rooms. Glass-fronted kitchen cupboards can seem to take up less space than solid doors. Open shelves are less formal, good for display, and easy to get at. Fewer cupboards will allow room for a painting or print, giving the room a more relaxed feeling.

WHAT TO CONSIDER

- Is there a good extractor fan—essential if eating in the kitchen to prevent strong cooking smells. ☐
- Have you chosen your kitchen storage specifically to hold the items you will have in your kitchen?
- Have you thought out the best lighting solution? There should be good general lighting and efficient light over work surfaces. ☐
- Have you thought of having open shelves rather than closed cupboards? They are less formal and can be more practical. ☐

A large extractor fan will draw even the strongest of cooking smells away from the dining area.

Deep storage cupboards create shallower storage between them—more convenient for small items.

The room divider is not just a visual barrier but provides a breakfast bar and coordinates both spaces.

A trolley on castors can be wheeled into either kitchen or dining room as required.

Although kitchen and dining area are divided, both areas are co-ordinated by wooden finishes and wooden furniture.

ARRANGING THE FURNITURE

- Measure the work area to make sure you can fit in the desk arrangement you would like to use.

- A small area, enough for a computer, will easily fit against a small area of wall. If you need more working area, an L-shaped desk can fit into the corner of a room.

- Arrange desk and chair then sit in the chair and perform some common tasks so you can be sure the arrangement is going to work for you.

- Check that there are convenient power sockets for phone, printer, computer, lighting, etc near the desk.

- If you use a drawing board a good place for it is directly under the roof light in an attic space.

- Anything related to the computer, such as paper or a scanner, should be within easy reach of your chair.

ARRANGING THE STORAGE

- Desks, filing cabinets, and cupboards can be fitted at low level, very like kitchen units, making a neat, workmanlike area.

- Storage for work probably needs to be more disciplined than leisure storage. You will need shelves, some sort of filing system, however primitive, and shelves or drawers the right size to take paper and envelopes.

- A plan chest is a better way of storing large plans than keeping them in rolls on top of a set of shelves. However, plan chests are usually enormous so make sure you can accommodate one.

- Divide shelving into compartments so that you know where everything is.

- A wall of shelving looks businesslike; keep it as close to the desk as possible.

- Store box files at medium height. They can get very heavy when full and are difficult to lift down from top shelves.

ARRANGING AWKWARD SPACES

- If two people are sharing and the work room is long and narrow, run a long, deep shelf as a desk along one wall and fit two people side by side rather than putting in separate desks for each person.

- In an attic the storage can be placed under the lowest part of the ceiling, with chairs and desk or table in the tallest part of the room where there is more head height.

- The space under a flight of stairs may be suitable for a small, custom-made workstation, but might work even better as a complete built-in office area with storage and desking conveniently arranged to suit your needs.

- In a dual-purpose space try to keep the office equipment to a minimum by keeping the storage at desktop height and the walls free for paintings or decoration.

- Purpose-designed work surfaces can be cut to fit awkward spaces.

The large windows are left uncurtained to let in maximum light in this artist's studio.

A long shelf is useful for storing the ingredients for still life paintings.

Basic furniture such as a trestle table and "found" items will not suffer from getting paint on them.

Ceiling pipes and plumbing have been left bare to allow the maximum room height.

A partition wall has created a narrow but useable space from the main room.

Trestles and a cut-to-fit table top provide a good painting surface right in front of the window.

CROSS REFER TO

- All day at home pp.14–15
- Homeworker/student pp.26–7 ● Entertaining pp.28–9 ● Dual-purpose rooms (dining/office, ktichen/dining, kitchen/office) pp.38–41 ● Landings and box rooms pp.56–7

CHOOSING FURNITURE

You can buy separate pieces of office furniture in many different designs and sizes and put them together individually, or you can have a work area purpose-designed and purpose-built. In between are myriad solutions, from fitting a modular shelving system with an extra wide shelf as your desk to a mobile desk-and-storage unit on castors offering everything you need in one piece of equipment. If you spend serious time at your computer you must have a supportive chair, preferably a purpose-designed typist's chair. Of course, other types of chair can also be perfectly satisfactory but to avoid RSI (repetitive strain injury) it's best to have one with height adjustment to allow you to sit with your feet flat on the floor and your arms at right angles from the elbow.

> "
> If you spend serious amounts of time at your computer you must have a supportive chair, preferably a purpose-designed typist's chair. It's best to have one with height adjustment.
> "

DESKS

• You will need a surface at least 30in (75cm) deep for a desk-top computer.

• A desk with built-in drawers, filing cabinet, and low pull-out shelf for the computer keyboard is practical.

• In a bed/work room a pale wood desk in a simple no-nonsense design, which could be mistaken for a dressing table, will co-ordinate well with other bedroom furniture.

• Modular office furniture is enormously flexible, giving you the choice of matching and co-ordinating desk, tables, chair, shelving, and filing systems, all in one look.

• If you are a tidy worker a put-away work station, enclosing your complete office paraphernalia, may be the answer in a dual purpose room.

• Mobile work units have everything you need, including the computer, scanner, VDU, and printer fixed to the one piece of equipment, and can be wheeled out of the way when necessary.

CHAIRS

- If you are going to buy a typist's chair, the back should lean inwards slightly to support the lower back, and be slightly flexible to allow you to lean back and stretch from time to time.

- Some people find kneeling chairs more comfortable than normal chairs, the idea being that you support your own back with your muscles instead of relying on the chair.

- Narrow chairs are available that take up less space.

- About 39in (1m) is considered a reasonable space between the desk and the chair, to allow you to pull it out and sit and work in comfort.

- Check that any arm rests don't prevent you from pulling your chair as close to the desk as is comfortable for you.

- Recommended features of a well-designed office chair include a wide back and shoulder support, curved seat front, and a wide, stable wheel base.

STORAGE

- Make sure all shelves, whether purpose-built or integral to a desk, are at suitable distances apart for the things you want to store.

- A built-in shelving system, perhaps integral to your desk, can be designed to take all your paper, envelopes, reference materials, and files.

- Books are heavy so make sure shelves are strong enough and well supported at frequent intervals so they don't bow.

- Most office paper and documents are standard size, so check that shelves and drawers are deep enough to take that measurement.

- In a dual-purpose room use pull-down blinds or doors to hide any untidy-looking shelves.

- Take into account the space required for large storage units in your initial plan, as they can be heavy to move around at a later date and the upheaval will interrupt your work.

Above This office, designed for two people, has a desktop running across the whole length of the room, making full use of the two large windows for light. Each person has his/her own storage and comfortable chair.

Left This room has been designed as much as a library or study as an office, as books predominate. The narrow space cleverly houses floor-to-ceiling bookcases, a desk in the window, and a luxurious upholstered armchair.

Bathroom

FITTINGS

The tiny spaces given to many bathrooms means they do present tricky design problems. Your scale plan will be invaluable when working out the best layout for the space and the most compact fittings.

The bath, shower, lavatory, bidet, and basin should be grouped fairly close together so they can share the plumbing outlets. This will decide to some extent the arrangement of the fittings. Built-in fittings often allow more room for boxed-in storage and give the room a co-ordinated look that will make it seem larger and give it a feeling of order. There are baths,

lavatories, and other fittings designed specifically to fit into small rooms—for example corner baths, corner lavatories, and corner basins are all available and are particularly suited to long, narrow bathrooms.

Corner equipment can make it possible, with some ingenuity, to create an extra downstairs or attic lavatory in a tiny cupboard-like space by using the whole of the width and length of the area and even to fit in a small amount of cupboard space round the basin.

WHAT TO CONSIDER

- Do you prefer a basin that looks like a Victorian wash bowl? ☐

- Have you got a bathroom radiator that doubles as a towel rail? ☐

- Do you prefer a free-standing furnished or a built-in look? ☐

- Have you considered using tongue and groove panelling, which can help insulate a cold bathroom and also co-ordinate the look? ☐

- Can you use the space between the bath and the end wall for storage? ☐

Very small chairs are available that will make a small bathroom more convenient and friendly.

A double-glazed roof light will make a small room lighter and can help to eliminate humidity and condensation.

Tongue-and-groove paneling on the walls helps to insulate and has a softening effect.

A round basin echoes the shape of the shower and also the old-fashioned feel of 19-century washing bowls.

A rounded shower cubicle not only saves space but also gives the appearance of more space.

"
Teenagers' needs are often very similar to students' requirements—that is, room for serious work and space for entertaining friends separately from the rest of the family.
"

YOUNG CHILDREN

- Cover radiators with radiator cabinets, which will not only protect the child from hot metal but provide a useful shelf for displaying small objects.

- Look in specialist furniture stores for versatile modular beds and storage items made especially for young children that can be arranged to suit the child's room.

- Bunk beds are good for two children but make sure the top bed is not too high for comfort and will allow the child to sit up.

- A raised platform for the bed can allow space underneath for a desk or for playing and storage.

- If a child's bed has drawers underneath, the top drawer at the head end can act as bedside storage.

TEENAGERS AND STUDENTS

- Invest in one piece of key furniture, perhaps a bed that incorporates lots of storage, and then spend less on soft furnishings.

- Try different configurations of beds and storage. A bed with a second pull-out bed underneath will be useful for sleep-overs.

- A low divan bed has an informal feeling and will double up as seating during the day. Check that the mattress remains firm at the edges when sat on. Cushions will come in useful as floor seating for friends.

- Insulate the floor and cover it with carpet if you want to protect the rooms below from loud music and heavy footfalls.

- A practical and pleasant desk/computer area is important to encourage homework and research. A long, wide shelf can make a good desk, but do add plenty of shelves for the CDs and general junk that collects around the computer.

ATTICS AND DUAL-PURPOSE BEDROOMS

- If the ceiling of an attic is at least 7½ft (2.3m) tall at the highest point it should be easy to turn it into a bedroom area.

- A low divan or day bed, covered with a throw or cushions, can be placed against the wall at the low part of the ceiling.

- In a dual-purpose bed/work room a desk can be made out of a shelf, fixed under the angle of the roof where the height of the wall will allow for sitting but not standing.

- Adapting shelving inside a wardrobe creates alternative storage that can be shared by both overnight guest and worker.

- Confine shelving and display space to a flat wall, leaving the rest of the room clutter-free.

- In a dual-purpose room a futon or sofa bed can put guests up overnight, then fold away when the rooms returns to office use.

Hobbies, toys, and games

Some hobbies require not only a working area but generous amounts of storage space as well, not unlike a home office. In fact, much the same advice applies except that your list of equipment and materials will require different sorts of storage and you should take this into account when designing the area. This may include activities involving a sewing machine, painting and drawing equipment, or model-making materials. Certain hobbies don't need a work surface in the same way as an office and materials and tools can probably be kept in a single workbox or basket. These include hand-sewing, embroidery, and knitting. Other hobbies might require numerous but tiny storage units, for example miniature drawers for housing beads, buttons, and other handicraft items. As with all your other planning, make a list of everything you use and then work out the most convenient and compact way to store them.

Your hobby may make good dual use of a spare bedroom or it may take place in a small corner of the living room. However, there are other activities that require a little more space. For example, woodworking makes a lot of mess. Ideally it should take place in a separate workshop away from the house, such as a garage or a garden shed.

WHAT TO CONSIDER
• Is your working table at a convenient height? ☐
• Have you plenty of storage suited to the materials you use? ☐
• Have you a chair or stool that does not give you backache? ☐
• Is the lighting efficient and without glare? ☐
• If you use flammable materials such as varnish or white spirit are they well protected? ☐

Good lighting is essential for craft or hobby work. Here, harsh strip lighting is diffused by glass panels.

Basic shelving systems will hold all the materials for your work, either separately or in boxes.

Sufficient floor space should be allowed for an artist to stand back and work at an easel.

A large waste bin is essential when doing any craft work.

A trestle table can be an ideal option for a work surface.

SEWING AND KNITTING

- Machine sewing is a hobby that takes time and constantly will be interrupted, so if you can leave it in place you will be able to pick up where you left off more quickly. However, as it needs a sizeable table, you may have to organize it so that you can pack it all away and get it out again easily.

- A neat and orderly way to keep yarns, sewing thread, small scissors, thimbles, etc in a miniature set of shallow drawers.

- A large pin or pegboard is excellent for keeping samples of fabric under your eye, where you can choose and compare textures and colors.

- You will need shelves for brochures, pattern books, and handbooks.

- Materials should be kept in a chest of drawers where they can be inspected regularly for signs of moth or beetle damage.

PAINTING AND DRAWING

- An adjustable drawing board or easel can be designed as part of a desk system, or be bought separately.

- A trolley can be wheeled to the most convenient position and carry all small items and equipment, such as pens, brushes, water, and varnishes.

- An attic is a particularly good room for drawing and painting because you get excellent light through a roof window.

- Portable equipment such as a folding easel and miniature watercolor paint box can be kept in a compartmented canvas bag on the back of a door.

- A pinboard and a slim portfolio are both good devices for looking at and storing finished artworks.

WOODWORK/DIY

- This sort of work is too noisy and dusty to be carried on conveniently in the main part of the home, but you could find space in a basement, garage, or shed.

- Organized tool storage is all-important because tools may be expensive, sharp, delicate, and dangerous. A large pegboard on one wall, marked with the shapes of individual tools, will keep them conveniently in place and easy to locate.

- You will need plenty of shelves, both shallow and deep, to hold different sizes of paint cans, nails, screws, glues, and varnishes.

- Specially designed miniature chests of drawers will keep small components separate.

- A portable workbench is practical, and excellent from the space point of view.

This room doubles as a sitting room and work room, so using one wall for work and storage makes good sense.

A laptop computer will take up far less space in a dual-purpose room than a desk model.

The natural colors and simple stripes on the sofa and window blind co-ordinate with the practical working area.

The tall shelves house all the working equipment that cannot be hung on the wall.

The trestle table has a white laminate top that is practical to work on and co-ordinates with the rest of the room.

CROSS REFER TO

- Lifestyle: the way you live pp.12–13 ● All day at home pp.14–15 ● Homeworker/student pp.26–7 ● Dual purpose rooms (dining/office, bedroom/office) pp.38–9 ● Understairs—open pp.50–1 ● Attics and basements pp.58–9 ● Work space pp.76–9 ● Essential small storage pp.102–3

TOYS AND GAMES

Adult pasttimes and games can take up almost as much space as children's, although they are usually less varied and need less categorized storage space. Either way, what's important is that they are kept where they are easy to find, easy to get at, and that there is somewhere convenient where they can be played. Dedicated games players may think it worth allocating a small room in the attic or basement for storing the computer and its accessories, as well as perhaps their collection of other games. A well-organized shelving system or cupboard will be adequate for storage, provided there is a suitable area or surface for playing.

> " Dedicated games players may think it worth allocating a small room in the attic or basement for storing the computer and its accessories, as well as perhaps their collection of other games. "

CHILDREN'S TOYS

- Young children like sitting in small chairs at small tables, and while they continue to enjoy this they take up far less space, so make the most of this short-lived time.

- A portion of one washable wall can become a large blackboard or painting surface. Children love painting on walls and it takes up less space than a blackboard and easel.

- Individual plastic boxes or baskets, lined up or stacking, can help to segregate different kinds of toys so you can separate the small and fragile from the large and sturdy. With any luck, the child will only empty one out at a time so there's not so much to put away at the end of the day.

- Computer games become a passionate interest for many children. Storage for disks should be within easy reach.

- A play area should have a warm floor covering, such as cork or carpet, to make it comfortable.

TABLE GAMES

- A kitchen or dining table makes a good surface for party and other games.

- For long-term games that may be interrupted by meals, such as board games or jigsaw puzzles, a lightweight folding table is more convenient. Card tables are perfect as they are designed for the purpose of playing games and become very slim when folded away.

- Games come in a motley variety of shapes and sizes, boxes and bags. You can store them satisfactorily in a living room cupboard but will need a carefully designed interior, with shelves of various heights and widths, if the game you want is not to languish under a pile of others.

- Keep a separate box of small bits, such as dice, scoring devices, paper, timers, and pencils, that can be used with any of the games.

TRAIN AND CAR SETS

- Train and racing car sets need a flat base or they won't run properly. Wood is better than a pile carpet—pile rugs can be moved before you play.

- If space is really at a premium it may be possible to fix the track or road permanently to a large board, which can be raised by a pulley towards the ceiling when not in use.

- Train and car sets are always bulky and difficult to put back into their boxes so keep the delicate bits—the cars and electrical parts—separate, where they won't get knocked about.

- Trains and racing cars often need a large area of floor space so make sure the surrounding furniture is lightweight or on castors and therefore easy to move out of the way.

- Make sure no valuable or vulnerable items are within breaking distance.

Above This cheerful corner of a child's room has a seascape mural and child-sized chairs around a table that is big enough three of four children to read together, or to play with bricks or board games.

Left This is a witty and highly efficient solution to keeping separate the numerous types of toys. There are large drawer compartments for train sets, dolls and their clothes, board games, and art and craft materials.

Large appliances

Refrigerator sizes vary, from small table-top models of about 1 cu ft (28 litres) to giants of 16 cu ft (452 litres). Don't choose a larger one than you need or you will simply waste electricity and space. An average family of four probably needs about 8.4 cu ft (424 litres) of refrigerator for foodstuffs they use daily.

When choosing a model, check the interior fitments. Accessories available include egg trays, cold-water dispensers, and bottle racks, and there may also be a "crisper" section to keep salad items cool but not too cold. Most refrigerators have doors hinged on the right, but some can be changed to hinge on the left.

When it comes to cooking appliances, in a smaller kitchen it makes sense to use separate components. A built-in oven can be placed at the most convenient height and the hob fitted separately, directly into the worktop.

Other large appliances include the washing machine and dryer. These are bulky items and it is often difficult to find a satisfactory space for them. If you can find a place outside the kitchen, such as a utility room, then so much the better.

WHAT TO CONSIDER

- Have you thought of a fridge with a mirrored surface, which reflects the room and seems to recede, not dominate? ☐
- Consider a small fridge and separate small freezer, rather than one large appliance. ☐
- Built-in units will allow you to incorporate cooking appliances into the cupboards, instead of a big floor-standing cooker. ☐
- Can you find a place for your washing machine and dryer outside of the kitchen? ☐
- Have you checked the interior of your chosen fridge to ensure it is suited to your needs? ☐

In a modern room a large, rectangular table can balance the bulk of a big fridge/freezer.

The circular mirror helps to balance the large geometric table and refrigerator, and makes the room appear bigger.

The very large stainless-steel freezer has a reflective surface that acts almost like a mirror.

A butcher block beside the fridge/freezer matches the kitchen units on the opposite wall.

The comfortable modern chairs fit in with the overall geometric feeling of this room.

REFRIGERATOR/FREEZER

- If you want a large freezer but don't have the height for a fridge/freezer, consider separate appliances under the worktop.

- A tall fridge/freezer can be built into your chosen kitchen units, which will make it seem more co-ordinated. Fit it at the end of a run of units where it won't dominate.

- If part of the kitchen is under the stairs you could use the tallest part of the space for storing a fridge/freezer.

- If your kitchen runs along one wall build a tall fridge/freezer on one end with a tall cupboard to match it at the other and create an alcove for the kitchen.

- Some fridges are designed to have a veneer panel on the front that matches the style of the kitchen, making them stand out less.

- A fridge/freezer fits happily next to a tall, narrow pull-out storage drawer designed to hold cans and dry foods.

WASHING MACHINE/DRYER

- If your kitchen is long and narrow use the length by creating a laundry area at one end. This can be divided from the kitchen area by a short peninsula, used for storage, or simply by a dividing partition.

- In a tall space a washing machine and dryer designed to stand one on top of the other will use the height and save floor space.

- Create a separate alcove for the washing machine/dryer by building cupboards around it. Make sure the space you choose is conveniently near existing plumbing.

- If you have a long, narrow bathroom you could build a compartment between the back of the bath and the end wall of the room to house the appliances. Check this conforms to safety regulations.

- You may be able to use a small area in the basement as a laundry, with an ironing board, linen cupboard, and airing space.

COOKING APPLIANCES

- You can choose a conventional all-in-one cooker or a separate cooker and microwave. Or you may prefer just one small tabletop appliance if you don't do much cooking.

- A separate oven offers great versatility but requires rather careful planning: you must decide whether you want the oven at eye-level or slightly lower down, and whether you want a stovetop with burners ranged along the back of the worktop or in the more usual four-square pattern.

- Some microwave cookers are combined with a conventional oven to form a versatile and space-saving all-in-one cooking unit.

- In a small kitchen where you don't expect to do much cooking you could consider having a plug-in grill, steamer, or casserole, and forego the oven altogether.

A built-in microwave oven is fitted into the ceiling-height cupboards as the low kitchen doesn't allow for much space on the worktop.

A large fridge/freezer provides a side wall to the worktop, creating a closed-in area.

All storage units are co-ordinated, including the front fascia of the fridge/freezer, giving a harmonious feeling to this kitchen.

The fitted cupboards have allowed space for a large extractor fan to remove unwanted cooking smells.

Oven and stovetop have been installed together, creating a compact cooking area.

Deep drawers next to the cooker provide enclosed storage for pans, lids, and other cooking equipment.

CROSS REFER TO

- Dual-purpose rooms pp.38–41 • Tall and narrow pp.42–3 • Tiny spaces p.46
- Creating a home pp.62–3
- Living and entertaining pp.64–5 • Eating pp.72–5
- Kitchen storage pp.106–9

WELL-THOUGHT-OUT storage is the key to living successfully in small spaces. It should be the framework to any arrangement and style you choose, and be one of the first considerations when doing your initial measuring and planning. Every single thing you own needs its own place, whether it's a case of wine, twenty pairs of shoes, or the electricity bill. Every item needs appropriate storage: many clothes should be on hangers, books should be kept upright, and tiny objects need their own separate space where they can be found and used when wanted.

You will need to go round your home making an inventory of everything you own. Then you can decide which objects will be best kept on open shelves and which behind doors. Storage needn't always be purely practical—decorative displays are also a form of storage. These can be on small tables, specially built shelves, or may be pictures on the wall. Letters and papers, passports, and photographs need some sort of filing system, even if only a series of box files. Above all, everything should have its own place and not be relegated to a nondescript cupboard.

Storage solutions

Storage types

Open shelving is one of the most versatile types of storage, acting as a way of displaying belongings, such as books and collected objects, with the advantage of being easy to see and to reach what you need quickly. Open shelving gives a greater feeling of space than enclosed cupboards, which bring the walls forward. There are various upright and bracket systems. Choose a sturdy one if you are going to store books and other heavy objects; make sure the shelves are strong enough to support the load and are themselves supported at regular intervals. Cupboards are also essential but must be well-organized inside and not used for concealing things you can't store elsewhere.

Cupboards and open shelves may be the mainstays of your storage strategy but there are other invaluable back-up storage devices to consider as well. Blanket chests, chests of drawers, stacking boxes, and rows of hooks or pegs are all invaluable.

And there are innumerable inventive small storage ideas, from long, narrow hall tables that double up as storage to miniature canvas or wicker wardrobes on castors.

An important part of your strategy should be how frequently you use particular items. Things used several times a day should obviously be easy to recognize and easy to reach. Things used once a year can be stored on tall shelves, but you should still be able to reach them safely with a set of folding steps. Heavy items should be stored where you can reach them and lift them without hurting your back. Cleaning equipment is often left out of the reckoning when planning storage and yet brooms, brushes, floor cleaners, cloths, and cleaning products take up plenty of space and are often very inconveniently jumbled into cupboards that are either too low or too high.

RECOMMENDED THICKNESS OF SHELVES AND DISTANCES BETWEEN SHELF SUPPORTS

MATERIAL	SHELF THICKNESS	DISTANCE BETWEEN SUPPORTS
Blockboard	½in (12mm)	18in (45cm)
Glass	⅜in (10mm)	27in (70cm)
MDF	¾in (18mm)	27in (70cm)
Melamine	⅝in (15mm)	16in (40cm)
Covered chipboard	¾in (18mm) 1¼in (32mm)	20in (50cm) 36in (90cm)
Plywood	¾in (18mm) 1in (25mm)	30in (80cm) 3ft 3in (1m)

GUIDELINES TO FIXING SHELVING

- Draw a plan of the wall to scale and mark the positions on the wall for the uprights or brackets with a pencil. Take care not to drill into any wiring.

- Melamine-covered chipboard may turn out to be more expensive than other shelving materials because it needs more support in the form of extra uprights and brackets.

- A strip of wood in front of thin shelves will give them a more substantial appearance.

- If you have partition or hollow walls, fix the shelving uprights or brackets to the timber uprights supporting the plasterboard at the back. These are usually 16–18in (40–45cm) apart. Find out where they are located by tapping gently with a hammer.

- Use special wall plugs or toggles to fix shelves to plasterboard, but note plasterboard take heavy weights.

- If you are fixing brackets or uprights to brick or plaster walls, fiber or nylon wall plugs will give the best grip.

Right Bookshelves need strong supports. Solid materials and thick shelves look best.

Left White is a good color for decorative displays as it emphasizes both color and shape.

Everyday storage

GENERAL

The things you use every day should be easy to see, easy to reach, and easy to put away again. You should not have to stoop or bend or climb on a chair to get at them, nor should you have to scrabble about among a chaotic jumble of other items to find them. Some form of open storage is usually the most convenient. Try to place the same size of object on a particular shelf so you don't space shelves further apart than you need for the sake of one large item.

A row of pegs can be useful for a motley collection of much-used items, such as outdoor coats, dog leads, and umbrellas. Rows of hooks screwed to the underside of kitchen shelves will take mugs, jugs, and cups, allowing more space in cupboards for things that won't hang up. Pegs fairly high up on the wall can also be used to hang folding chairs – an old Shaker solution for storing furniture.

Something not often considered is the storage of rubbish and other items waiting to go elsewhere, and yet they are really a part of everyday life. There are better ways of coping with these than the ugly black plastic bag waiting for pick-up day.

Some form of open storage is usually the most convenient. Try to place the same size of object on a shelf so you don't space shelves further apart than you need.

Left A basket with a handle can be a convenient store for items such as toys that you may want to move from one part of the house to another. This one has been woven to fit over the stair tread.

Below This simple piece of furniture takes up little space but will hold a telephone, mobile phones, books, letters, and boxes for such items as postage stamps or pens.

CLOTHES

- Arrange the interior of your clothes cupboard with great precision for clothes used everyday, with both hanging and shelf space.

- A pack of stiff but flexible drawer dividers will give you separate spaces in a chest of drawers for socks, underwear, ties, and other small items.

- Include a shirt rail for short clothes, leaving space below for pull-out shelves.

- Divide shelves into separate areas to take jerseys and other foldable clothes.

- Hang ties and scarves over expanded curtain wire, and belts by their buckles from hooks fixed to the inside of cupboard doors.

- Freestanding mini-wardrobes of canvas or rattan, containing hanging storage, shelves, and pockets, can greatly help to organize day-to-day storage of clothes if you have no room for a full-size wardrobe.

- Don't forget to declutter at least twice a year. Nothing fills up with worn out goods as quickly as a clothes cupboard.

TEMPORARY STORAGE

- Make sure you have a large enough kitchen waste bin to last until collection day. If it does fill up too early, keep a clear space at the bottom of the broom cupboard for short-term storage of full rubbish bags.

- Keep charity bags near the front door where they will not be confused with rubbish bags and get thrown out.

- Make sure any hall table has a shelf you can keep empty for books waiting to be taken back to the library or to be passed on to friends.

- If there's no room for a table in your entrance hall, fix a very narrow shelf for mail and books, or fix a narrow box or basket to the wall.

- Dirty laundry can be a problem, and if there is nowhere to put it it will lie around in heaps in the bedroom and bathroom. A swing bin as part of fitted bathroom furniture will solve this problem, but if there's no room then a spring-up net basket can be put out of the way when not in use.

MISCELLANEOUS ESSENTIALS

- Fix a narrow shelf with a row of hooks inside the front door to hold the house and car keys.

- If the electricity meter is in the hallway, build or fix a neat little cupboard round it and keep a flashlight in there in case of emergencies.

- If there is no electricity meter in the hall, fix a narrow shelf fairly high on the wall but still within reach to store the flashlight, etc.

- A narrow console table can look good in a hallway. One with shelves or compartments is absolutely invaluable for mail in and mail out, stamps, a pen, and many other much-used items.

- Make sure there are enough towel rails in the bathroom for everyone in the house. There is nothing more depressing than a soggy towel with nowhere to be aired.

Above A well-designed and organized space can be created by fitting sliding transparent doors at the end of a room or side of a passage. A high-level clothes rail leaves room below for storage of linen.

LIVING ROOM

Above all other storage in your house, living room storage should reflect the style of your home as well as providing convenient housing for all your belongings. Your list of things to be stored will include everything from television and entertainment equipment, disks, and videos to books, magazines, photos, collected objects, and more. Nor should you forget the bills and other paperwork involved in everyday living. It may be that you have a desk in the living room and would like to keep your filing system in here as well. You can design and tailor this storage entirely to your own requirements but there are many modular systems and freestanding storage items that may fit in even better with the style of your home.

Left A large library of books can be difficult to house. Here most of the available wall space, including the area above the door, has been shelved.

Right Storage can be both organized and decorative, as shown by this attractive "wheel" of CDs mounted on the wall.

Far right An attractive, no-nonsense filing trolley with purposeful castors can be a good answer to keeping papers in order within a small home.

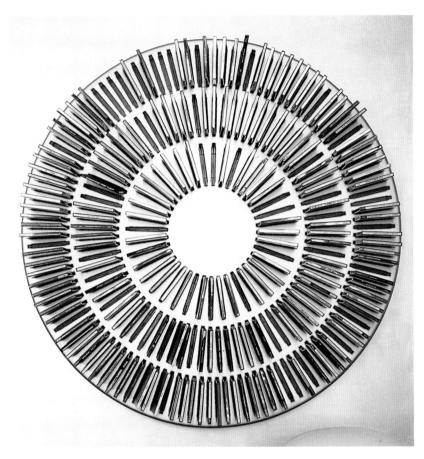

BOOKS

- Bookcases should be suited to the books you own. Don't waste space installing deep shelves if all you have is paperbacks.

- If you want to graduate the shelves, start with the deep ones at the bottom and move up to narrower ones.

- Make sure you have enough shelving so that books don't have to be squeezed in tightly, which will damage them.

- A combination of shelves and slightly wider cupboards underneath can be very practical and look attractive too.

- A coffee table with a glass top and a shelf underneath will store large books that can easily be taken out and enjoyed.

- Don't conceal bookshelves with a large chair or sofa. What you can't see, you will soon lose interest in or forget about.

PAPERS AND FILING

- You may not need to access your papers every day but it's vital that you can find them quickly and easily when you need to.

- It's best to categorize your papers and keep them in separate compartments or files. Categories could include unpaid bills, letters awaiting replies, car papers, bank papers, school correspondence, and addresses.

- Letter-size files are suitably sized, available in good, bright colors, and look smart lined up on a shelf.

- A concertina file can be a good answer for all family paperwork.

- A small traditional or modern bureau will allow you to keep all your filing in the one piece of furniture.

CDS AND DISKS

- Any shelf used for disks should be only as deep as the CDs themselves, otherwise they get pushed too far back against the wall and are difficult to reach and organized.

- Upright column racks for CDs can stand in any narrow space and are available in many different styles, from traditional wood to modern metal.

- A freestanding horizontal storage unit can sit on an existing shelf.

- A series of specially designed canvas CD holders can be stored on top of one another, and if you categorize them carefully you can easily find the CDs you want—perhaps to take with you when travelling.

- The most often-played CDs are best stored at eye level so that you can see what you want without having to pull out dozens of disks before you find it.

Essential small storage

When de-cluttering drawers you may be able to chuck out most items, but you will be left with a small core of essential items that you don't want to put back into the drawer where they will get lost again among incoming jumble. Every day there are moments when you might want to seal a package with tape, sew on a button, or put a new battery in your camera. These are all small items easily lost among the plethora of other objects littering drawers in the home, yet when you do want them you want them in a hurry. Finding individual storage spaces for them really saves time and tempers from fraying, and there are lots of possible solutions.

Above A radiator shelf encourages the heat to go out into the room and can be invaluable for storage. The enormous pegboard is an inspired way of displaying pictures and photographs, creating a mini art gallery.

Top right A set of shelves designed like the top half of a dresser can house a collection of china; this one has useful drawers for miscellaneous items such as napkins. Cup hooks are invaluable for mugs and jugs.

PIN AND PEG BOARDS

- A large peg board with hooks is a convenient home for scissors, reels of sticky tape, paint brushes, balls of string: in fact, anything small and light enough to hang.

- A pin board is great for phone numbers, bills waiting to be paid, addresses, and contacts.

- A pin board is also excellent if you have a hobby, for sample materials or yarns, details of suppliers, sketches, and samples of work.

- A pin board makes a good reference area for any home decorating, as you can compare paint colors and fabric samples.

- Hang the board in an accessible position, near to the place you will usually need it.

- If you often use items in separate rooms, hang two boards and double up on the items they hold. This can save a lot of frustration and pacing back and forth.

MINIATURE DRAWERS AND COMPARTMENTS

- Miniature sets of workshop drawers designed for nails, screws, and wall plugs of different sizes can be invaluable for all sorts of miniature objects, from paper clips and staples to batteries and picture hooks.

- More stylish miniature drawers in cardboard or acrylic are also available, perhaps more suited to a home environment. They can be a good way of sorting things you use in sewing, such as buttons, needles, embroidery scissors, and ribbons. They probably won't last as long as the more workmanlike workshop ones but are certainly pretty and practical.

Make sure the drawers open and shut
smoothly.

- Slightly larger drawers in sets of three or
six are available in unfinished wood so you
can paint them to match your own décor.
Use them to store such items as address
labels, rolls of parcel or carpet tape, a
spare phone, a small camera, various
adhesives, colored inks, or what you will.

MISCELLANEOUS

- Sets of different-sized pockets of storage
to hang on a wall can be the perfect
answer to miscellaneous storage. Canvas
sets of pockets are available in various
configurations and sizes. Something like
this can be good hanging on the back
of the kitchen door for holding small
gardening equipment such as trowel,
string, scissors, dibber, secateurs, wire
rolls, wire cutters, and seeds.

- A sturdy hanging-storage device made
of moulded plastic pockets, designed
in the 1960s, has a strong retro look
and can be used as much as a sculpture
as for storage. Items like this are better
suited for small office or hobby storage
such as pens, pencils, brushes, rolls
of tape, household scissors, and so on.

- Many items can be hung from a section of
rod-and-hook storage above the worktop
in the kitchen. Although usually used for
mugs you can also hang scissors, keys,
or anything with a handle in the same
way.

- Divide a kitchen drawer (you can buy
compartments for drawers) to take
specific small items. However, this will only
work if you are disciplined about what you
put in the drawer.

Right Bookshelves fixed high up on the wall, reached
by an elegant ladder, leave room underneath for a
sound system. The modular seating and fluffy rug are
designed to promote comfortable listening or reading.

Long-term storage

Items that you won't want to use for six to 12 months and can afford to put away can be put in more inconvenient places than everyday storage, but where they will be safe from dust, moths, or accidental knocks. When putting clothes away for a season you should wash them or have them dry cleaned them first. Clothes need to "breathe" and should never be so tightly packed that they become permanently creased. Cover them with plastic or pack them in separate plastic bags to protect them from moths. If you fold them carefully they will take up less space. Place tissue paper between the folds and between the individual garments.

Clothes are not the only things that hang around waiting to be used. Baby and child equipment, such as cots, strollers, and tricycles, can all take up far too much unnecessary space waiting for the next baby or simply because you don't know what to do with them. The best solution for these is to find somebody else who would like them—a local charity shop if no friend or relative decides to have a baby. Other possible items for long-term storage are luggage and old wedding-photograph albums that you only take a look at once or twice a year when friends or relations come to stay.

Right This clever bed has a cantilevered mattress base that can be raised to reveal storage for a variety of items, from small boxes to spare duvets and pillows.

Bottom right This display of shelves and pegs is an adaptation of a Shaker idea. Originally intended for chairs and other furniture, it can hold a variety of objects for show or for occasional use.

Below This consciously sparse bedroom stil has room for storage in the large cabin trunk at the end of the bed and the elegant armoire.

CLOTHES

- A blanket chest can be useful storage for seasonal clothes, and has the advantage of being an attractive piece of furniture you could keep in a hall or living room.

- The top of the wardrobe can be used for storing clothes but the boxes or bags you keep them in should be airtight to prevent moths and dust getting in.

- Any hanging clothes for the next season should be covered in sealed plastic bags.

- Cardboard hat boxes or plywood Shaker boxes make attractive storage for hats or other items you want to put away safely.

- Always wash clothes or dry clean them before storing, as moths are far more likely to be attracted to dirty clothes.

LARGE OBJECTS

- Outgrown baby strollers, cradles, and cots can take up an inexcusable amount of space. Either find temporary borrowers until you need them again, or throw them out.

- Outgrown toys in good condition should also be given away or lent to friends. Toys take up an enormous amount of space, so don't keep any that are not being used.

- If you want to hold on to a bike to pass on to another child you may be able to fix a bracket to a wall in a hall or passage to hang the bike on, or fix it to a pulley on the ceiling.

- A large travelling trunk, as with a blanket chest, need not be hidden away but can itself be used as long-term storage for clothes. Cover it with an attractive rug and it can double up as seating.

- Bulky equipment, such as a projector for the occasional viewing of slides or an old-fashioned record player for listening to LPs, can be put in a drawer under the bed or on top of the wardrobe.

MISCELLANEOUS

- You may find space for family archives, old diaries, and correspondence in box or other files among your day-to-day papers, but they do take up space. A useful way of creating discreet extra storage for such objects is to build a shelf above a door.

- Old photographs, wedding videos, and other things you don't want to get rid of but will seldom refer to can also be housed on a tall shelf or a shelf above a door.

- Travel luggage is often in the form of squashable bags, in which case it shouldn't be too difficult to squeeze into a convenient space. A small wheely suitcase can be used to store squashy bags inside, but the larger the case the more difficult to store. On the whole luggage is not particularly beautiful, so hidden storage is best. Under the bed, on top of the wardrobe, a top shelf of the wardrobe, or at the top of the linen cupboard are all possibilities.

Kitchen storage

Kitchen storage is probably the most complicated in the home. Cooking itself involves so many different stages and tools and pieces of equipment, all different shapes and sizes, many of which you want to be able to get at and use at a moment's notice. Planning the storage for all these objects begins with the original measurements and plan of the kitchen as a whole, the way you move around in it, and the most convenient placing of the larger items such as the refrigerator/freezer and oven.

Once the basic kitchen has been designed, you can begin to plan the detailed storage for individual items. Because of the sheer numbers and complexities of the items to be stored, it's a good idea to start with a checklist. You can add to this any items you feel are important. There are basically three types of storage useful in a kitchen—hanging storage, shelves (open or enclosed), and drawers—but there are one or two ingenious and unusual ideas for storing certain difficult items.

CHECKLIST

ITEMS TO BE STORED

- Pans and lids ☐
- Plates and dishes ☐
- Mugs and cups ☐
- Glasses ☐
- Cutlery and utensils ☐
- Vases, jugs, large bowls ☐
- Cooks' knives ☐
- Trays and roasting tins ☐

Above Plastic-coated wire shelves enable organized storage of many more items than if they were all jumbled up together.

Right Stainless-steel rods and hooks are extremely versatile. Here several rods have been fixed to a swivel panel, making the pans easily reached by the cook.

BEDLINEN

- Cupboards or shelves near the hot water tank are invaluable. Modern insulated tanks do not let much warmth escape but the cupboards will still be convenient and dry for storing bedlinen.

- If you have been able to create an alcove in an interior part of your home for a laundry area there should be room for generous shelving, and this is an ideal space to house all items that can be ironed and put away promptly.

- If you have room for specially designed bathroom fitments, and your bathroom does not suffer too badly from condensation or get too damp from hot baths and showers, shelf space can be found for spare towels and bath mats, releasing space elsewhere in the home for bulkier items such as spare curtains. (Perhaps spare curtains should have gone out with the clutter though!)

- Don't keep any extra items that you really don't need. Most sheets these days can be washed, dried, and put back on the bed the same day.

- Fitted sheets will not fold into quite the same neat squares as conventional sheets, but take up little space nonetheless.

TABLE LINEN

- A couple of tablecloths and a set of table napkins don't need to take up much space so a kitchen, dresser, or sideboard drawer should be able to cope with all your table linen.

- Of course, if you have a linen cupboard then make the most of that. Provided you keep all the items neatly folded, you will be able to fit in a surprising number of items.

- If you are lucky enough to have space for an old-fashioned decorative armoire in the hall or kitchen then that's the ideal place for storing linen—it's what armoires were invented for in the first place. Small, modern versions are often fitted with chicken wire in the doors so they are ventilated and airy.

- The airing cupboard is not necessarily the best place to store table linen as constant warmth discolors linen and can eventually weaken the fibers.

MISCELLANEOUS

- Many of the throws and rugs draped over furniture will be in use much of the time so won't need storage space. However, there are often one or two spares, especially travel rugs, that you will seldom use. Travel rugs can be left in the car.

- Attractive extra blankets, rugs, and throws can be folded and laid on the end of a bed to save storage space elsewhere.

- Spare duvets, rugs, blankets, and other items that take up a lot of space can be stored in a drawer compartment underneath a bed. Take them out and shake and air them from time to time.

- Spare cushion covers are unlikely, in reality, to be used again and the same is true of spare curtains. Find another home for them or throw them away.

> "Household textiles are not necessarily in use all the time but may be needed at a moment's notice when friends come to stay or you are giving a dinner party."

MAKING THE MOST of a small home or small spaces in the home is a challenge, but there are plenty of cunning tricks to help make your home seem larger than it actually is. You can use paint and pattern, light and reflection, highlight architectural features, and lead the eye away from confined spaces and along vistas to interesting objects or intriguing glimpses of another room. Be consistent: use the same color to coordinate flooring in different areas and rooms. Be adventurous: use changes of color to emphasize a flight of stairs or another extension of the space.

Don't be afraid of white, which reflects light better than any other color and always makes a room seem larger. Be inventive: frame a window with a good view by painting a different color around it. Be creative: Use paint techniques to give an impression of depth, or different patterns to add to the feeling of height. Make use of dado and picture rails, friezes, deep skirting panels, and arches to emphasize height. Keep some wall space clear for a favorite painting or print. And, of course, declutter: too much furniture and too many objects will cramp a room uncomfortably.

HIGHLIGHTING ARCHITECTURAL FEATURES

- Highlighting architectural features will lead the eye through and give a spacious feel.

- A small room will seem larger if the interior is flooded with soft light from wall lights or lights shining downwards.

- Cove and cornice lighting, with specially designed fitments that run under the cornice, give a soft and gentle light that blurs the boundaries of a room.

- Highlight an alcove by concealing one or more lights in the arch or ceiling above it.

HIGHLIGHTING PICTURES AND OBJECTS

- Picture lights are attached to individual works and are most practical for lighting pictures no taller than 2ft (61cm), otherwise the bottom of tall pictures can remain unlit. They do bring a picture to life and, if the rest of the room is not too bright, greatly diminish any "enclosed" feeling.

- An adjustable spotlight recessed into the ceiling can spread a broad beam of light over a large painting.

- Sculptures and bowls or vases can be lit with a spot lamp from below or above.

- Plants with architectural foliage look spectacular lit from below, but remember that plants need daylight in order to flourish. If there is limited light, use special "daylight" bulbs to ensure the plants receive enough ultraviolet light.

- Books are very seductive, so use wide-angle spot lamps to light a bookcase from an angle, thus emphasizing the effects of shadow and texture.

- Glass objects on glass shelves can be lit from underneath with low-voltage tungsten-halogen spotlights, or from behind with tiny, wall-mounted fluorescent strips to diffuse light through a translucent screen of semi-opaque glass or muslin.

Use of mirrors

Mirrors are often underestimated as sources of light and extenders of space, and are used merely as a way of checking appearance. In fact their effects can be magical. They can open up dark corners, illuminate gloomy basements, and not only create illusions of space but also provide optical surprises. A large, well-placed mirror can almost double the amount of light in a room if opposite a big window, and that in itself always makes a room seem larger. They can be particularly effective in narrow halls and corridors where they can seem to double the width. When hanging a mirror try to get someone to help you by holding the mirror in place so you can see what it is reflecting and where it best works in the way you intended. Always make sure the mirror reflects something attractive—there's no point in reflecting a dull wall with nothing on it or an open door leading to nowhere interesting.

“ A large, well-placed mirror can almost double the amount of light in a room if opposite a big window, and that in itself always makes a room seem larger. ”

DARK AND NORTH-FACING ROOMS

• In north-facing rooms use bright, pale colors, such as yellows, to bring in a warm, sunny feeling.

• Use apricots, scarlet reds, and oranges to cheer up rooms that receive little daylight.

• In a deep basement, where light has to filter down from street level, reinforce your cheerful light colors with daylight bulbs and plenty of mirrors to reflect both color and light.

• Alternatively, accept the situation and create a cozy, cavelike interior with warm reds and several low-level lamps.

ECCENTRIC SPACES

• Use a decorative paint finish, such as stippling or distressing, to soften the edges and give the walls a subtle feeling of depth.

• Paint a very high ceiling in a darker color, picking out any ceiling mouldings, roses, cornices, and so on in white.

• Warm colors such as reds and oranges will appear to bring the ceiling closer.

• A dark-colored floor to reflect a dark ceiling will appear to "connect" the two, making the height seem less in a tall room.

• Paint one wall a different color to the others to make a narrow space seem wider.

DEALING WITH DETAILS

• Pick out good-looking architectural features in white or a positive color, and really make the most of door architraves, stair balustrades, plaster details, and so on.

• Highlight a pleasant view by framing the window in a contrasting color. Paint it to look like an actual frame or simply paint a wide band of solid color around it.

• The kitchen and bathrooms can be given a matte finish rather than the usual gloss. It seems less institutional, but is still washable.

• Decorative paint techniques such as dragging, stippling, and distressing can give walls textural interest and a 3D look.

• A sunny, light room can take cool colors as the daylight will bring them to life.

Use of pattern

Patterns can be used creatively to alter the proportions of a room. Whether a pattern is large or small, formal or informal, or highly colorful or monotone can have enormously different effects on the final result. Limiting the pattern to certain sections of a wall or part of the room can also be helpful in defining areas. A simple geometric pattern may be easier to live with than a large overblown floral, which can add to the feeling of clutter in an already busy room. Plain colors and patterns can go well together, provided there is a common color to link them. The main color of a pattern can be picked up as the paint color in a room, or you can achieve more subtle effects by selecting an inconspicuous color in the pattern and using that as the main paint color. Highlighting the secondary color gives further opportunities for using it in soft furnishings such as curtains and cushions.

Left You can mix patterns, but they should have a unifying factor—here the enormous flowers on the right echo the smaller ones on the left and the stripes of the hand-woven rug echo the colors of both.

Right In this bold room the wide and narrow stripes on the wall are complemented by the pattern created by the logs waiting to be burned, which are in turn echoed by the pattern on the folded rug under the table.

STRONG PATTERNS

- Strong patterns, as with strong colors, appear to come forward and will make a room seem smaller.

- The linear quality of vertical stripes or a checkered pattern can maximize the sense of height in a room.

- Choose a stair carpet with strong border stripes to lead the eye upwards. This works particularly well in a small hallway.

- If you use vertical stripes to accentuate the height of a low room, follow through by using similar stripes or checks on chair seat covers or cushions to achieve a look that is co-ordinated and restful.

- Stripes and checks can complement each other, but don't choose too wide a stripe or too large a check, which will dwarf the room.

SMALL PATTERNS

- Small, overall patterns will blend in with the rest of the room but may seem a little too "busy" in a living room.

- A small bathroom can be made warmer and more friendly with a small floral all-over design on one wall.

- Neat and pretty geometric or floral papers can help to conceal the variations in height in the slope of an attic ceiling.

- A tiled border will smooth the transition from tiles to plastered wall in a small bathroom.

MISCELLANEOUS

- Staircase walls and landings benefit from consistent use of one color and pattern throughout to make them harmonious.

- Choose patterns that will fit into the context of your home style: florid Victorian designs will look odd with minimalist furniture, and large "loud" patterns can diminish a small space even further.

- If you are dividing a wall horizontally with a dado or curtain rail, choose a pattern for just one of the areas and plain color for the rest.

- Monotone patterns, such as blue-on-white Toiles de Jouy or buff-on-white, may be more restful than full color in a small bedroom.

Curtains and blinds

Curtains can be used to keep out inquisitive eyes, to frame a good view or conceal an ugly one, to soften the contours of a room, or to conceal shelves where doors would take up too much space. They can also be used to create a feeling of enclosure or privacy when used around a bed, for example, or to divide a room. They can certainly be used to accentuate a particular style—heavy and draped for a Victorian-style living room, or light and airy for a modern bedroom. As far as pattern on curtains and blinds is concerned similar guidelines apply as for patterned wallpaper, but there are specific ways you can use curtains and blinds that can be helpful in dealing with small spaces.

"

Curtains and blinds can be used to accentuate a particular style— heavy and draped for a Victorian-style living room or light and airy for a modern bedroom. „

CURTAINS

- Floor-length curtains look generous and help give a unified look to a tall room. Curtains that end just below the window sill look more cottagey and suit smaller windows.

- Carry the curtain pole well beyond the extent of the window itself to make sure you can draw the curtains right back and let in as much light as possible.

- If you want a light, informal look have unlined curtains in a sheer fabric, such as muslin or organdie.

- A curtain under a single child's bunk will screen the play space underneath, allowing privacy and concealing any mess.

BLINDS

- Wall-to-wall windows are difficult to screen because it's unsatisfactory having curtains that can't be drawn away from the window completely. Two or three roller blinds in a row can be pulled right up to the top of the window, and will not keep out any light.

- Roman blinds, which pull up into large pleats, are both decorative and elegant—suitable for creating an uncluttered look.

- Venetian blinds with narrow slats can be particularly useful for a work space where they can be adjusted to prevent glare from full sunlight.

- Roller blinds present the simplest look of all and can be used with curtains if wanted.

MISCELLANEOUS

- Fix roller or slatted blinds to sloping attic windows, with hooks at the bottom to prevent them from falling vertically.

- A muslin or organdie coronet can give an ordinary bed a luxurious feeling without taking up much extra space.

- Muslin draped over a divan against the wall can add immediate elegance without wasting space.

- Screen shelves fixed under a basin with crisp gingham or other cotton fabric to conceal their contents.

Above Venetian blinds are a very good choice for windows that are overlooked or that get too much sun at certain times of day. They always look neat, but can be adjusted to let in more or less light as required.

Left Sheer curtains running along the whole length of a wall can be drawn right back from the window to allow all the available light into the room. They are useful to filter the light at the brightest time of the day.

Screens and dividers

A screen separating one area from another can be invaluable in a room used for two or more purposes. This can be as heavy-duty as a built-in room divider in the form of open shelves or cubes, or as minimal as a small three-panel folding screen to create a psychological barrier as much as a physical one. A screen can be placed on runners to slide open or fixed in one place. It can be light and airy, as in lightweight portable Japanese shoji screens consisting of a lightweight wooden frame and translucent paper with three or more panels. Or it can be as important for its storage as for its screening qualities, creating the effect of two separate rooms but without losing the sense of space.

Portable folding screens can be useful in screening off, for example, a work area or clothes storage without altering the proportions of the room. They vary enormously in style so you could choose a simple bamboo screen, a Victorian collage, or a modern "designer" screen. Even such a small portable piece of furniture as a screen can give the sense of privacy that a completely open space cannot.

Right This wall screen is similar to a Japanese shoji screen, which divides up the spaces in a home while allowing light through. Some can have sliding doors, others can be free-standing. The transparent panes of glass make the space seem more generous.

Above The simplest screen made from fabric (in this case a sheet of canvas) hung from the ceiling can provide enough privacy for two young children to share a room while retaining their own separate spaces.

Right Gauze strips hung from the ceiling can provide an attractive screen between one part of a living area and another, while still allowing light through. Such a screen is as much psychological as visual.

FOLDING SCREENS

• A folding screen can be used in a child's room to provide a private space for baby bathing and changing. It can be fitted with hooks for hanging tiny clothes.

• The most basic screen can have panels covered in your choice of fabric, thus blending into the room, and in a bedroom it can be used to hang clothes on.

• Modern folding screens in sculptural shapes and bold, colorful designs will complement a modern interior and screen off a work station.

• Use folding screens not only as a way of concealing things, but as a way of displaying textiles or a collection of antique clothes perhaps.

FIXED SCREENS

• Japanese shoji screens can run along grooves fixed to the floor and ceiling and be drawn aside at will, thus creating one room out of two, or vice versa. Shoji screens are also available as free-standing units that will screen off an area of a room. They are light-weight so can be moved around if needed.

• Built-in open storage shelves or cubes make good storage from either side, as well as screening one part of a room from another, effectively creating two separate areas.

• Sliding/folding doors can be used to divide two rooms, but make sure they are made of narrow panels or they can be awkward and take up too much space when opened out.

• In a kitchen a peninsula unit can create a room divider at worktop height, or extend upwards to form a screen made of shelves or cupboards opening on both sides.

MISCELLANEOUS

• Textiles can be used effectively to screen off a dining table or a living room from a computer desk. Run curtain track where you want the hanging, and leave it un-gathered. This makes an inconspicuous but definite division of the area without taking up too much space.

• Ready-made muslin or other sheer curtains are available in white and a variety of colors, perfect for screening off a bed or a section of a room discreetly.

• Glass bricks can make an excellent screen to divide a shower from the rest of the bathroom, an en-suite bathroom from the bedroom, or a laundry area from the cooking area in a long, narrow kitchen.

Resources

United Kingdom

B&Q plc
tel 0845 609 6688
www.diy.com
low cost, flat pack kitchen, bathroom, bedroom furniture and flooring

Bisque Ltd
244 Belsize Rd
London NW6 4BT
tel 020 7328 2225
www.bisque.co.uk
stylish and inventive radiators and towel rails

C P Hart
Newnham Terrace
Hercules Road
London SE1 7DR
tel 020 7902 5250
www.cphart.co.uk
stylish bathroom and kitchenware

Christopher Wray, 591–593
Kings Road
London SW6 2YW
tel 020 7751 8701
www.christopher-wray.com
traditional and contemporary lighting, furniture and accessories

The Cotswold Company Ltd
1 Apollo Rise
Southwood
Farnborough GU14 OGT
tel 0870 241 0973
www.cotswoldco.com
furniture and soft furnishings

Crabtree Kitchens
17 Station Road
Barnes
London SW13 OLF
tel 020 8392 6955
www.crabtreekitchens.co.uk0
range of bespoke handmade kitchens

Estia Component Furniture
Unit 12 South Close

Orchard Road
Royston SG8 5UH
tel 01763 252920
www.estia.co.uk
modular office furniture

Fired Earth
3 Twyford Mill
Oxford Road
Nr Banbury OX17 3SX
tel 01295 812088
www.firedearth.com
furniture, bathrooms, flooring, paints

The Futon Company
168–169 Tottenham Court Road
London W1T 7NP
tel 7636 9984 (for other branches call 0845 609 4455)
www.futoncompany.co.uk
futons, curtains, furniture, accessories

Habitat
196 Tottenham Court Road
London W1T 7PJ
tel: 020 7361 3880
www.habitat.net
furniture and home accessories

Heals
196 Tottenham Court Road
London W1P 9LD
tel: 020 7636 1666
www.heals.co.uk
contemporary upmarket furniture and accessories

The Holding Company
241–245 Kings Road
London SW3 5EL
tel 020 7352 1600
www.theholdingcompany.co.uk
stylish, inventive contemporary storage for home and office

IKEA Brent Park
2 Drury Way
Neasden
London NW10 OTH
tel 0845 3551141

(11 branches in England and Wales)
www.ikea.com
furniture, kitchens and accessories

John Lewis
Oxford Street
London W1A 1EX
tel 020 7629 7711
www.johnlewis.com
everything for the home

Lakeland Ltd
Alexander Buildings
Windermere LA23 1BQ
tel 01539 488100
www.lakelandlimited.co.uk
small storage solutions and accessories

London Lighting Company
135 Fulham Road
London SW3 6RT
tel 020 7589 3612
www.londonlighting.co.uk
wide range of modern lighting

Magnet Ltd
Brazen House
27 Great Ancoats Street
Manchester M4 5AJ
Tel 01619234994
www.magnet.co.uk
kitchen units and appliances

Marks and Spencer plc
Waterside House
35 North Wharf Road
London W2 1NW
tel: 020 7935 4422
www.marksandspencer.com
living and bedroom furniture and accessories

Royal Institute of British Architects
66 Portland Place
London W1N 4AD
tel 020 7580 5533
www.riba.org
can give names of local architects and can advise on using an architect

USA

Alternative Closet Company
74 North Industry Court
Deerpark NY 11729
tel 1 800 698 2444
www.alternativecloset.com
*custom-tailored adjustable
storage system*

American Council for an Energy
Efficient Economy
1001 Connecticut Avenue
NW Suite 801
Washington DC 20036
tel 202 429 0063
www.aceee.org
*provides information on the energy
efficiency of household appliances*

American Institute of Architects
1735 New York Avenue
NW Washington DC 20006-5292
tel 202 626 7300
www.aia.org
*information on working with an
architect and lists of local architects*

Bedroom Furniture USA
7517 Quiet Cove Circle
Huntington Beach
CA 92648
tel 866 888 3058
www.bedroomfurnitureusa.com
wide range of furniture

Big Apple Futons
240 East 23 Street
New York, NY 10010
tel 212 481 1171
www.bigapplefuton.com
*futons, platform beds, storage beds,
loft beds*

Brand Lighting Showroom
873 SW 30th Avenue
Hallandale FL 33009
tel 954 456 1006
www.brandlighting.com
all kinds of lighting and shades

Crate & Barrel
725 Landwehr Road
Northbank
Illinois 60062-2393

tel 001 847 2888
www.crateandbarrel.com
*traditional and contemporary home
office furniture and storage*

Coleman Furniture
1800 Sherwood Forest
Houston TX 77043
tel 281-652-5944
www.colemanfurniture.com
*very wide range of furniture for the
home at good prices*

Elgot Kitchens
937 Lexington Avenue
New York NY 10021
www.elgotkitchens.com
tel: 212 879 1200
*cabinets, countertops, appliances,
plumbing fixtures, remodelling service*

Europea Home Furnishings
6231 West Dempster
Morton Grove
Illinois 60053
tel 847 967 1977
www.europafurniture.com
European designer furniture

Haiku Designs
PO Box 4673
Boulder CO 80306
tel 1 800 736 7614
www.haikudesigns.com
*Japanese furniture including platform
beds and screens*

IKEA Twin Cities
8000 IKEA Way
Bloomington MN 55425
tel 952 858 8088
(36 stores across the USA)
www.ikea.com
*everything in modern Scandinavian
design for the home*

L L Bean Flagship Store
95 Main Street
Freeport ME 04033
(11 stores and outlets in USA)
tel 800 559 0747
www.llbean.com
*furniture and accessories for
the home*

National Kitchen and Bathroom
Association
687 Willow Grove
Hackettstown NJ 07840
tel 800 843 6522
www.nkba.org
*supplies basic consumer information
about remodelling kitchens and bathrooms and will help find local members*

Neiman Marcus
737 North Michigan Avenue
Chicago IL 60611
(plus six showrooms)
tel 312 642 5900/800 642 4480
www.neimanmarcus.com
home furnishing, beds and bedding

Pier 1 Imports Inc.
100 Pier 1 Place
Fort Worth TX 76102
tel: 817 252 8000
www.pier1.com
attractive informal furniture

Schneiderman's Furniture Store
17630 Juniper Path
Lakeville MN 55044
(plus six stores in Minnesota)
tel 952 435 3399
www.schneidermans.com
*wide range of traditional and modern
furniture for the whole home*

Swartzendruber Hardwood Creations,
at The Old Bag Factory
1100 Chicago Avenue
Goshen Indiana
tel 800 531 2502
www.swartzendruber.com
living, dining, office furniture

Tema Contemporary Furniture
7601 Montgomery NE
Albuquerque NM 87109
tel 505 683 8362
www.tema-usa.com
contemporary furniture and lighting

The Conran Shops
Bridgemarket, 407 East 59th St.
New York NY 10022
tel 212 755
9079 www.conran.com
designer furniture home accessories

Index

Acknowledgments

Mitchell Beazley would like to acknowledge and thank all the following agencies, photographers and companies who have provided images for use in this book.

Key: a above, b below, l left, r right

1 New England Shutter Company, www.tnesc.co.uk, contact info@tnesc.co.uk; 2 Andreas von Einsiedel/interior design Gerard Conway; 4 Narratives/Jan Baldwin/design Rita Koenig; 7 Andreas von Einsiedel/interior design Gareth Smith; 8l see 15, 8r see 17, 9l see 23, 9r see 27; 11 Redcover.com/Winfried Heinze; 12l Camera Press/Marie Claire/Marie Pierre Morel/Marie Kalt; 12r Ray Main/Mainstreamimages; 13 Camera Press/Marie Claire Mason/Paul Lepreux/Catherine Ardouin/Caroline Tine; 15 Camera Press/Schoner Wohnen; 17 Narratives/Liz Artindale; 19 Octopus Publishing Group/Dominic Blackmore; 21 Silent Gliss, www.silent-gliss.co.uk, contact info@silentgliss.co.uk; 23 Narratives/Viv Yeo; 25 Redcover.com/Verity Welstead; 27 Photozest/H&L/S Calitz; 29 Redcover.com/Huntley Hedworth; 30l see 58, 30r see 47, 31l see 39, 31r see 43; 32 Redcover.com/Verity Welstead; 33 Camera Press/Home; 36l Interior Archive/Simon Upton/architect Block Architecture; 36r Photozest/Dook/H&L/architect John Radford for Q&N; 37 Photozest/Inside/L Wauman, architect F Orban; 38 Narratives/Jan Baldwin; 39a Camera Press/Living at Home; 39b Corbis/Beateworks/William Geddes; 40 Redcover.com/Guglielmo Gavin/design Carden Cunietti; 41 Redcover.com/Simon McBride; 42 Narratives/Jan Baldwin; 43 Interior Archive/Luke White/design Jibby Beane; 44 Interior Archive/Luke White/architect David Kelman; 45 Redcover.com/Henry Wilson; 46 Photozest/H&L/M Hoyle; 47l Ray Main/Mainstreamimages; 47r Ray Main/Mainstreamimages/design David Tansley; 48 Camera Press/Paul Massey; 49 Camera Press/Brigitte; 50 EWAStock.com/Andreas von Einsiedel; 51a Camera Press/Femina; 51b Andreas von Einsiedel/design Reinhard Weiss; 52l Narratives/Jan Baldwin; 52r Bisca, www.bisca.co.uk, contact info@bisca.co.uk; 53 EWAStock.com/Andreas von Einsiedel; 54 Photozest/Inside/T Jeanson; 55l Corbis/Beateworks/Andrea Rugg; 55r Redcover.com/Niall McDiarmid; 56 Narratives/Jan Baldwin/artist Erica Van Horn; 57 Redcover.com/Paul Massey; 58 Redcover.com/Huntley Hedworth; 59 Redcover.com/Mark York; 60l see 76, 60r see 75, 61l see 83, 61r see 64; 62-3 Redcover.com/Huntley Hedworth/architect Mike Mcrae; 64 Narratives/Jan Baldwin/architect MM Architects; 65 Interior Archive/Fritz von der Schulenburg/Cath Kidston; 66l Interior Archive/Fritz von der Schulenburg/architect Nico Rensch; 66r Bowers & Wilkins, www.bwspeakers.com; 67 Redcover.com/Graham Atkins-Hughes; 68 EWAStock.com/David Giles; 69 Camera Press/Zuhause Wohnen; 70 Camera Press/Home; 71l Camera Press/Tuis; 71r Oslo kitchen by Stoneham, www.stoneham-kitchens.co.uk, engineering by Blum, www.blum.com; 72 Interior Archive/Fritz von der Schulenburg/architect Nico Rensch; 73 Camera Press/Marie Claire Maison/Eric Flogny/styled by Catherine Ardouin; 74 Redcover.com/Henry Wilson/design Mick McMahon; 75 Redcover.com/Johnny Bouchier; 76 Camera Press/Zuhause Wohnen; 77 Photozest/Inside/S Anton/decor by Eugenie Collet; 78 Narratives/Jan Baldwin/design Charlotte Crosland; 79 Photozest/H&L/D Chatz/architect Aurelio Cimato at MCM Architects, South Africa; 80 EWAStock.com/Di Lewis; 81 Redcover.com/Winfried Heinze; 82l Narratives/Polly Wreford; 82r Redcover.com/Jake Fitzjones; 83 EWAStock.com/Bruce Hemming; 84 Interior Archive/Simon Upton/design John Wright; 85 Camera Press/Schoner Wohnen; 86 Narratives/Polly Wreford; 87 Photozest/H&L/Ryno; 88 Redcover.com/Reto Guntli; 89 Photozest/Inside/J Hall; 90 Redcover.com; 91 Narratives/Jan Baldwin/design Grant White; 92 Redcover.com/Dan Duchars; 93 Opus kitchen by Stoneham, www.stoneham-kitchens.co.uk, using Blum engineering, www.blum.com; 94l see 102, 94r see 99, 95l see 97, 95r The Holding Company, www.theholdingcompany.co.uk, contact mail@theholdingcompany.co.uk; 96 Redcover.com/Chris Tubbs/design Nikki Tibbles; 97 Redcover.com/Chris Tubbs/design Samantha Robinson; 98a & b The Holding Company, www.the-holdingcompany.co.uk, contact mail@theholdingcompany.co.uk; 99 Photozest/Inside/L Wauman/stylist C Exelmans; 100 Interior Archive/Tim Clinch/designer Clare Nelson; 101l Camera Press/Marie Claire Maison/Benedicte Ausset; 101r The Holding Company, www.theholdingcompany.co.uk, contact mail@theholdingcompany.co.uk; 102l Redcover.com/Paul Massey; 102r Redcover.com/Brian Harrison; 103 Redcover.com/Dan Duchars; 104 Redcover.com/Andreas von Einsiedel; 105a Ocean, www.ocean-furniture.co.uk; 105b Redcover.com/Mark York; 106l Redcover.com/Mike Daines; 106r Nolte Kitchens, www.nolte-kuechen.de, contact email@noltekitchens.co.uk; 107 EWAStock.com/Rodney Hyett; 108a AEG Electrolux, www.aeg-electrolux.co.uk, contact aeg-hausgeraete.kundenservice@aeg-hausgeraete.de; 108b Fisher Paykel, www.fisherpaykel.co.uk, contact sales@fisherpaykel.co.uk; 109l & r Photozest/Inside/B Claessens; 110 Redcover.com/Dan Duchars; 111l Orga-line by Blum, www.blum.com, contact info@blum.com; 111r Neff, www.neffweb.com, contact neff@neffkitchens.com; 112 Photozest/Inside/I Snitt; 113a Redcover.com; 113b Redcover.com/Lucinda Symons; 114l Villeroy & Boch, www.villeroy-boch.com; 114r Narratives/Jan Baldwin/design Malcolm Kutner; 115 Red Cover/Paul Massey; 116l see 137, 116r see 121, 117l see 129, 117r see 123; 119 Narratives/Polly Wreford; 120 Andreas von Einsiedel/interior design by Candy & Candy; 121 Photozest/Inside/M Roobaert; 123 Redcover.com/Tom Scott/design by London Furnishing Co; 124l Redcover.com/Tim Evan-Cook; 124r Redcover.com/Dan Duchars; 125 Redcover.com/Simon McBride; 126l Ray Main/Mainstreamimages; 126r Baikal mirror by Aram, www.aram.co.uk, contact aramstore@aram.co.uk; 127 Mainstreamimages/Darren Chung; 128 Ray Main/Mainstreamimages/Pearl Lowe; 129 Ray Main/Mainstreamimages/Mathmos; 130 Redcover.com/Brian Harrison; 131 Narratives/Jan Baldwin; 132 Redcover.com/Mark Williams; 133 Redcover.com/Dan Duchars; 134 Redcover.com/Grey Crawford; 135 Silent Gliss, www.silentgliss.co.uk, contact info@silentgliss.co.uk; 136l EWAStock.com/Michael Crockett; 136r Redcover.com/Winfried Heinze; 137 Ray Main/Mainstreamimages.